John White Geary

Message of his Excellency John W. Geary to the General Assembly of Pennsylvania

John White Geary

Message of his Excellency John W. Geary to the General Assembly of Pennsylvania

ISBN/EAN: 9783337399856

Printed in Europe, USA, Canada, Australia, Japan

Cover: Foto ©ninafisch / pixelio.de

More available books at **www.hansebooks.com**

OF

HIS EXCELLENCY

JOHN W. GEARY,

TO THE

GENERAL ASSEMBLY

OF

PENNSYLVANIA,

JANUARY 8, 1873.

——— ———

HARRISBURG:
BENJAMIN SINGERLY, STATE PRINTER,
1873.

MESSAGE.

*To the Senate and House of Representatives of the Common-
wealth of Pennsylvania:*

GENTLEMEN:—In obedience to the requirements of the
Constitution I have the honor of transmitting to you my
sixth annual message. Since your last meeting the general
course of events, both State and National, has been so propitious as to afford abundant cause for mutual congratula-
tion, and of thanksgiving to that Almighty Providence whose
will controls the destinies of all. While we have been exempt
from the calamity by fire that has befallen the metropolis of
a great sister State, her misfortune has inured to the benefit
of our people by the enlistment of that sympathy for the suffering which is one of the most ennobling sentiments of the
human heart. The seasons, though not so favorable for the
productions of our soil as in some past years, have been sufficiently fruitful; and no general epidemic has appeared to
disturb the pursuits, or fill with sorrow the hearts of our
population. Our mining industries, manufactures and internal commerce are being constantly enlarged and extended,
and their enterprising proprietors are generally receiving remunerative returns.

A great political conflict has occurred, resulting in a signal
triumph of the same principles that were asserted in the
restoration of the Union, the amendments of the Constitution, and the reconstruction of the States. The victory in
Pennsylvania was decisive of the victory in the Nation; and
will ever be remembered as an inestimable contribution to
the harmony, prosperity and glory of the country. The elec-

tion of the soldier, who "is first in war," to the office that makes him "first in peace," was an appropriate exhibition of national gratitude, and inspires the deepest feelings of satisfaction "in the hearts of his countrymen."

While the Constitution wisely withholds from the Governor all power of interference in legislation, it imposes upon him the duty of laying before the General Assembly such information of the state of affairs, and recommending to their consideration such measures as he may deem expedient and important to the public welfare.

I am happy to inform you that peace and good order have been maintained by the enforcement of just and equal laws, and the legitimate exercise of authority continues to find an enduring basis of support in the intelligence, affections and moral sense of the people.

FINANCES.

The credit of the State remains unquestioned abroad, because her public faith has been inviolably maintained at home. The following condensed statement of the receipts, expenditures and indebtedness of the Commonwealth is respectfully submitted:

Receipts.

Balance in Treasury November 30, 1871	$1,476,808 50
Ordinary receipts during the fiscal year ending November 30, 1872	7,148,637 45
Total in Treasury during year ending Nov. 30, 1872,	$8,625,446 04

Disbursements.

Ordinary expenses paid during year ending November 30, 1872	$2,960,631 55	
Loans, &c., redeemed...............	2,476,326 00	
Interest on loans paid..............	1,706.032 88	
Total disbursements..........		$7,142,990 43
Balance in Treasury November 30, 1872............		$1,482,455 61

Public Debt.

The public debt on Nov. 30, 1871, was, $28,980,071 73
Add Chambersburg certificates 299,748 91
Add Agricultural College Land Scrip
    fund, held in trust, as per Act ap-
    proved April 3, 1872 . . . .   500,000 00
                     ————————$29,779,820 64
Deduct amount paid by Commissioners of the Sink-
    ing Fund during the year ending Nov. 30, 1872 . . . 2,476,326 00

Public debt, November 30, 1872 . . . . $27,303,494 64
Deduct assets in Sinking Fund $9,300,000 00
And cash balance in Treasury 1,482,455 61
   Amount of assets and cash . . . . ————————$10,782,455 61

Balance of public debt unprovided for $16,521,039 03
which can be extinguished in ten years by the annual payment of
one million six hundred thousand dollars.

During the last six years payments on the debt have been
made as follow:
Amount paid in 1867 . . . . . , ... $1,794,644 50
   Do . . . . 1868 . . . . : 2,414,816 64
   Do . . . . 1869 . . . . 472,406 18
   Do . . . . 1870 . . . . . : 1,702,879 05
   Do . . . . 1871 . . . . 2,131,590 17
   Do . . . . 1872 . . . . 2,476,326 00

   Total payments $10,992,662 54
Being a little over *twenty-nine per cent.* on the debt due De-
cember 1, 1866, which was then $37,704,409 77.

Sinking Fund.

In remarking upon this subject, I trust it will be instruc-
tive to refer, briefly, to some of the facts relating to the accumulation and payment of the public debt, and the origin of
the assets arising from the sale of the public improvements.

However wise our predecessors were in opening avenues for trade and commerce, and however great were the benefits resulting to the people from the internal improvements of the State, it is obvious, that while those of other States rarely failed to become sources of revenue, the management of ours was such as to produce results widely different. A large majority of the tax-payers, therefore, after long and patient endurance, becoming dissatisfied with their management, demanded they should be sold; assuming it would be a measure of economy, and would prevent an increase of the public obligations.

The construction of the improvements resulted in a public debt, which, in 1852, reached its maximum, $41,524,875 37. The interest, premiums and other expenses that have been paid upon the debt, from its incipiency to November 30, 1872, sum up $76,845,744 99; and make the entire expenditure on account of the public works, $118,370,620 36.

In pursuance of law the State canals and railroads were sold in 1857, for eleven million dollars in bonds; upon which the State has received $1,700,000 00 in cash, and $9,300,000 00 remain in the hands of the Commissioners of the Sinking Fund, as follows, viz:

Bonds of the Pennsylvania Railroad Company, secured
  by lien on the Philadelphia and Columbia Railroad, $5,800,000 00

Thirty-five bonds of the Allegheny Valley Railroad
  Company, each for $100,000, guarantied by the
  Pennsylvania Railroad Company, Northern Central
  Railway Company, and the Philadelphia and Erie
  Railroad Company, payable $100,000 annually, be-
  ginning January, 1875, bearing 5 per cent. interest
  from January 1, 1872 ....   3,500,000 00
                                                  ─────────────
    Amount of assets 9,300,000 00
                                                  ═════════════

Remarks on the foregoing Financial Statements.

The proper and efficient management of the finances is one of the most important duties of the administration of the State government. The collection of the revenue; the economical expenditure; the safe keeping of the public moneys, and well-guarded appropriation bills, are always questions of deep interest to the tax-payers of the State.

It is a lasting honor to the people of Pennsylvania, that they have never, even when struggling under the most oppressive burdens, permitted the integrity of the State to be doubted, and now it cannot be otherwise than gratifying to them, to learn the rapid extinguishment of the public indebtedness, the greater part of which was incurred for improvements, which, as herein already shown, utterly failed to be advantageous to her coffers.

The rapid reduction of the State debt, and the reduction of taxation, have gone hand in hand throughout my entire administration, and have constituted a marked portion of its policy, attesting, at the same time, the concurrence and wisdom of the Legislature, and the fidelity of those who have been the custodians of the public funds.

This policy should be continued, and no attempt to cover up or conceal the actual expenses of the government should be made for the purpose of obtaining the people's consent to appropriations, or enterprises of doubtful propriety; which propositions, if coupled with a condition to raise the money by immediate and direct taxation, would be unhesitatingly rejected.

The Legislative appropriations, during the last six years, made in aid of the various institutions for the support of the deaf, dumb, blind, insane, feeble-minded, friendless, wanderers, orphans, soldiers' homes, hospitals, universities, houses of correction, penitentiaries, and the payment of military expenses, incurred during the war; expenses of government,

·common schools, and soldiers' orphans' schools, amount to about $17,000,000 00.

The expenses of the soldiers' orphans' schools alone, during the same time, is $3,467,543 11, and, although it is a most noble and patriotic expenditure, it is, nevertheless, an unusual one, and if such a necessity had not existed, the reduction of the State debt, during their existence, would have been nearly fifteen million dollars.

During the past six years, the current of legislation has been steadily in favor of reduced taxation. Not only have numerous local laws been enacted, exempting churches, cemeteries, schools, hospitals and other institutions from taxation, but many general laws of the same character have been passed, as is shown by the following enumeration:

By the "act to amend the revenue laws," approved, February 23, 1866, all real estate in the Commonwealth was thereafter made exempt from taxation for State purposes.

By the act approved March 30, 1866, all persons who served nine months or upwards in the military service, or who were honorably discharged therefrom by reason of wounds or physical disability contracted therein, and their property, were exonerated from all bounties, and *per capita* tax and military fines.

The act of April 29, 1867, repealed all laws requiring payment of taxes to the State on sales of loans and stocks by auctioneers.

By the act of April 10, 1867, all trustees, or owners of property to the value of thirty-five thousand dollars, used for soldiers' orphans' schools, were exempted from all "county, road, city, borough, poor and school taxes."

By the act of April 4, 1868, and the supplements thereto, "all mortgages, judgments, recognizances, and moneys owing upon articles of agreement for the sale of real estate," were made "exempt from all taxation, except for State purposes."

By act approved January 3, 1868, all laws therein recited were repealed, which imposed taxes upon "the shares of stock held by any stockholder in any institution or company. incorporated under the laws of this State, which in its corporate capacity is liable to, and pays into the State Treasury the tax on capital stock imposed" by the acts therein recited.

The act of June 2, 1871, repealed so much of the law of April 29, 1844, as imposed a tax of two per cent. on salaries. trades, offices, occupations and professions.

And by the act of April 3, 1872, the sixth section of the law of April 21, 1854, was repealed, which imposed a tax of one-half of one per cent. on the capital stock of all corporations created under laws "to enable joint tenants, tenants in common, and adjoining owners of mineral lands, to manage and develope the same."

In view of these facts, the practical questions now are, can any further reductions be properly made? And if so, on what subjects?

Heretofore on several occasions I have invited the attention of the Legislature to the importance of adopting a more liberal policy towards those citizens who are engaged in industrial enterprises which employ large numbers of workingmen, and tend to develop the resources of the Commonwealth. Involving great risks, and requiring for their successful conduct a large amount of capital, these operations have been, in the main, conducted by means of associations, organized under the general laws which regulate the incorporation of manufacturing, mining and improvement companies. These laws, while they resemble in their principal features the liberal systems in force in other States, fail in their ostensible purpose of encouraging manufacturing industry, because the privileges they grant are enormously burdened with taxation.

This may be illustrated, by supposing the case of twenty persons, who each subscribe five thousand dollars to the stock of a company organized for the purpose of producing oil, or mining ore or coal, or manufacturing cotton or woolen goods, iron or steel, or any other commodity. The fund thus created must be expended in lands, buildings and permanent improvements, *which are taxable for all purposes to the same extent as if they were owned by an individual operator.* In addition to this the company must pay a *bonus of one-fourth of one per cent. to the Commonwealth upon its stock amounting to the sum of two hundred and fifty dollars.* It is thereafter liable to an annual tax upon its capital stock at the rate of *one-half mill for each one per cent. of dividends made or declared.* In case of no dividends having been made or declared, *then three mills upon the appraised value of the stock.* Also, *a tax of three per cent. upon the entire amount of net earnings or income.* Also, *a tax of five per cent. on all interest paid to bondholders and other creditors.* (For all these taxes, see act of May 1, 1868.)

An individual, wealthy enough to furnish a hundred thousand dollars in similar business, would be wholly free from these exactions. The State imposes none of these burdens upon him. It does not keep an espionage upon his business, or demand from him sworn statements of his annual profits. It discriminates in his favor against the association of small capitalists which it professes to encourage. And without sharing in any of the stockholder's risks, it makes itself a partner in their profits and follows them with a grasping hand, and a never-ceasing official vigilance of an inquisitorial character over their affairs.

Such conditions are unknown to the laws of New England, New York and other rival manufacturing States, which, without exception, carefully prohibit duplicating of taxes upon their own industry. Stock in manufacturing companies is generally taxed by them at its value, like other personal property, but first the value of all real estate represented by the stock is deducted, and made taxable like the property of other individuals in the region where the lands are located. It is by such liberal provisions that these States have fostered their industries and maintained a monoply of capital and supremacy in manufactures.

The western and southern States, for many years our customers, are beginning to be our rivals : and desiring to draw to themselves the benefits flowing from diversified industry, they are enacting the most liberal laws for the encouragement of corporate and individual efforts to establish manufactories, and in addition to this, towns and cities are giving large subsidies to secure the erection of mills and factories within their limits. Notwithstanding the discovery of large bodies of coal in the western States, and their close proximity to vast masses of pure ores, Pennsylvania would still possess at least equal, if not superior, attractions for the investment of capital, were it not for her oppressive tax laws ; all of which have a tendency to drive capitalists beyond her borders to seek locations less burdened for their investments.

Nothing but very strong necessity could justify such a variety of taxes upon the same thing. And if any justification ever existed, I believe it to exist no longer. The time has come when, with proper diligence in collecting and economy in expenditures, the State can well afford a reduction of taxation ; and legislation in that direction should be such as to relieve the undue burdens of taxation from every form of productive industry. I would, therefore, recommend that the enrolment tax upon private acts chartering industrial companies, and the bonus upon stock of such companies when organized under general laws, be considered a full equivalent to the Commonwealth for the privileges of a charter; and that all State taxes upon capital stock, net earnings and dividends of manufacturing, mining and improvement companies, and all co-operative associations, be repealed. This reduction will amount to $549,554 23—the sum collected last year. I also recommend the repeal of that source of revenue known in the Auditor General's report as "Tax on Loans," which amounts to $492,407 28.

It is confidently believed that with these proposed reductions, which amount to $1,041,961 51, the State can still pay all her current expenses, the interest on the public debt, and make an annual reduction of at least one million five hundred thousand dollars upon the principal.

GEOLOGICAL SURVEY.

Numerous communications, signed by many enterprising and intelligent citizens, continue to reach me, on the subject of a geological and mineralogical survey, urging me to commend it to your careful consideration.

In my annual messages of 1870 and 1871, I laid before the General Assembly the necessity for a continuation of the surveys already made, in order that the mineralogical resources of the State should be more fully and perfectly ascertained; and expressed the opinion that the results would be interesting and valuable, not only to our citizens individually, but to the entire country.

Assurances have been given by the officers of the "United States Coast Survey" of the great interest they will take in our State, in the event they carry out their intention to cross the continent to connect the "Ocean lines of Coast Surveys." This connection will pass through Pennsylvania, and will materially assist in determining and establishing one or more points in each county through which the line will pass, aid in triangulating so far as to enable us to rectify our county maps and connect them in a correct map of the State. And as the State Geologist progresses with his studies and examinations, he should cause to be accurately represented upon the corrected maps, by colors and other appropriate means, the various areas occupied by the different geological formations, and place them in the possession of the people, for their information, prior to the completion and publication of a full account of the survey.

A State map of the kind indicated, with all the discoveries marked in proper colors thereon, would give to the thousands of visitors from our own country and from foreign lands, who will attend the Centennial celebration, some approximate idea of the incalculable wealth beneath the soil of our State; and would have an importance in their sight that could be conveyed to them in no other possible manner.

The expenses of a geological corps, properly organized, and such as would be competent to perform the duties required, have been carefully estimated, and will not exceed forty-five thousand dollars for the first year, and need not be quite as much annually thereafter. In recommending this measure two years ago, I said: "For want of a proper bureau of statistics, and a corps of observation and publication to collate and relate the facts of our geology and mineralogy as they have appeared, the State has already suffered severely. Much valuable information has been lost, never to be recovered; and but little certain knowledge of past mining, and other scientific operations, has been preserved to govern and assist the future engineer. It is, therefore, neither wise nor just policy to delay this work under the pretext that it may be more perfectly effected at some future time. There is a present necessity for it, though the time never will come when such a work can be considered perfect. New developments in mineral resources, as well as additional acquirements in scientific knowledge, will constantly be made as long as the world exists. The sooner, therefore, in my opinion, a thorough survey is authorized, the better it will be for the prospective interests of the State, as well as for its present necessities."

The golden destiny of the Pacific States may well be envied; but our coal, ore, oil, lumber and soil are a much better foundation for wealth and permanent greatness than the products of all their *placers*, and the transient prosperity they have produced. Let us build upon an enduring basis and the world will forever pay a golden tribute to our products and industries—the true wealth of Pennsylvania.

BUREAU OF LABOR STATISTICS AND OF AGRICULTURE.

By an act approved April 12, 1872, establishing a "Bureau of Labor Statistics and of Agriculture," the Governor was authorized to appoint a Commissioner of that Department. Accordingly Thomas C. Macdowell, of Dauphin county, was appointed. He immediately established his office in the Capitol building, as required by the act, and commenced the work of collecting the necessary information and arranging the statistical tables, in proper and convenient form to be laid before the Legislature, and for distribution among our citizens.

The functions of the commissioner embrace the examination of nearly all the varied industries of the State, and are defined in the act as follows: "The duties of such officer shall be to collect, compile and systematize statistics, with reference to the subject of labor in its relations to the social, educational, industrial and general condition, wages and treatment of all classes of working people, and how the same affect our permanent prosperity and productive industry. It shall also be the duty of such Bureau to collect, collate and classify statistics relating to the mineral, manufacturing, agricultural and commercial productions of this Commonwealth." The fourth section makes it the duty of the chief of such Bureau to report annually to the Legislature, in convenient form, the result of his investigations.

The act does not appropriate any money to defray the necessary contingent expenses of putting the Department in working order, nor does it prescribe the manner of obtaining the information required, or that it shall be furnished; and it leaves the commissioner without any means by which he can obtain it, except by the voluntary act of those engaged in business. These were evidently over-sights which will doubtless be corrected by an appropriation, and by the passage of such enactments as will enable the commissioner to procure, from the proper sources, the information required to carry out the intent and meaning of the law.

When it is remembered that Pennsylvania ranks second in population; second in manufactures; sixth as a wheat growing State, and first in point of mineral wealth and resources, among the States of the Union; it should not be a question of dollars and cents, whether her vast and varied resources shall be left to be developed by the slow process of casual discovery, or be properly introduced to the notice of capitalists at home and abroad, by authorized and official statements of facts.

The information that will be furnished, will not only be of great practical value to the citizens of the State, but it will afford the representatives of the people, who are charged from year to year with the responsibilities of legislation, the best and most compendious source of information, the importance of which can only be estimated by experience.

Pennsylvania stands pre-eminent for her mineral resources, possessing, as she does, the only known anthracite coal fields, of any consequence, whilst her iron ores, and oil are a source of inexhaustible wealth, that defies computation. A few items only are necessary to prove the correctness of these remarks. The production of coal, from the anthracite regions, in 1820, was 365 tons; in 1870 it reached the enormous amount of 19,951,585 tons, and it is estimated that the product will be swelled in 1872, to upwards of 22,000,000 tons. If the increase in the production of anthracite coal has been so rapid and wonderful in a period of fifty-two years, who can estimate its growth within the next half century? The product of our bituminous coal fields, in 1870, foots up 14,968,465 tons. The two make an aggregate of 34,920,050 tons for that year.

Meanwhile, the development and growth of the oil production of the north-western counties, almost challenges the credulity of our people. From August, 1859, when Drake

sunk the first well, to the close of 1864, the production was
221,000,000 gallons, yielding the sum of $29,820,000. In
1864, about 62,000,000 gallons were refined, the average price
of which, in bond, at New York; (sixty-two cents per gallon,)
gave a value of $38,440,000. The entire production, up to
1868, was 327,692,524 gallons, equal to 8,493,339 barrels of
crude oil.

There is no doubt the future reports of the commissioner
will disclose an equally rapid increase in the production of
oil, and other facts concerning it not less gratifying.

The remunerative prices paid at present for pig metal is
inducing the erection of a large number of first class fur-
naces, which will materially increase the wealth of the State,
and give a new impetus to other branches of business dependent upon their products for active and profitable results in
the near future.

There are other questions of much interest to the public
welfare, which can only be evolved with any degree of cer-
tainty by careful investigations ; such as those affecting the
health, comfort and general well-being of the people, but more
especially the industrial classes, who are the main dependence
of the State for its continued prosperity. The question of
labor, in all its relations, is one that constantly engages a
large share of attention, and the subject can only be intelli-
gently and properly legislated upon, after the researches of
the statistician are laid before the Legislature, with such accompanying testimony, as will reduce to a demonstration the
abuses which exist in our social system. Much might be said
in this connection, but your patience shall not be unduly
taxed by more extended observations, as I am confident the
question of labor, in all its relations, cannot fail to engage
the serious attention of enlightened and patriotic representatives.

In view of all the facts connected with the Bureau of Statistics, I most earnestly bespeak for it liberal appropriations,
as well as the fostering care of the Legislature.

CONGRESSIONAL APPORTIONMENT.

On the night prior to the adjournment of the Legislature
at its last session, a bill was submitted for my approval ap-
portioning the State into Congressional districts, for the period of ten years, under the national census of 1870. The
enactment was highly objectionable in many of its features;
and Congress then had under consideration a supplemental
bill proposing an increase of representatives, that would give
one additional member to this State. This afterwards became a law, thereby giving to Pennsylvania twenty-seven
members of Congress instead of twenty-six, as provided for
in the legislative enactment of the last session. The latter
having failed to receive Executive approval, the Congressional elections last October were held under the former law, and
the three additional members apportioned to the State were
chosen as members at large by the vote of the whole people.
Hence, the duty of enacting another apportionment bill devolves upon the present Legislature, and I request for it that
careful and patriotic consideration required by the magnitude
of the interests involved.

STATE TREASURER.

The sixth section of the sixth article of the Constitution
declares that—

"A State Treasurer shall be elected annually by joint vote
"of both branches of the Legislature."

But the Legislature, by joint resolution, passed at two con-
secutive sessions, and approved by popular vote at the last
October election, has amended this part of the Constitution,
by striking out the section above quoted, and inserting in
place thereof the following:

"A State Treasurer shall be chosen by the qualified electors of the State, at such times and for such term of service
as shall be prescribed by law."

2

The adoption of this amendment will be officially proclaimed on the second Tuesday of January, 1873, and will supersede existing laws for the election of State Treasurer by the Legislature. Inasmuch as no provision seems to have been made by law for filling this office, from the first Monday of May next until an election can be had by the people under the amended Constitution, I invite the attention of the Legislature to this condition of the subject, and recommend such action as will carry out the amendment, and in the meantime secure so important an interest of the Commonwealth.

CONSTITUTIONAL CONVENTION.

The several duties imposed upon the Executive and Secretary of State, by the act of the last session authorizing the convention, were duly performed. The delegates having been chosen at the October election, convened in this city on the twelfth day of November. The convention, after completing its organization, appointing its standing committees, and adopting rules for its government, adjourned to meet at Philadelphia on the seventh of the present month.

A careful revision of our fundamental law is imperatively demanded by the highest considerations of public welfare; and it is confidently hoped the action of that body may be such as to meet the just expectations of enlightened public opinion.

SANCTITY OF THE BALLOT-BOX

Many of the laws now upon our statute books were designed to fortify the ballot-box against corruption and fraud, but practically they have often been rendered impotent for that purpose, and even for the prevention of false returns. Numerous complaints have been made to me on this subject by many highly respectable citizens, who have requested that I would, once more, urge it upon the attention of the Legislature, and ask the passage of more stringent enactments for

the suppression of such crimes against the rights of the citizen. Redress for these wrongs is expected from the Constitutional Convention, and it is hoped the public expectations
will be realized. It is believed, however, the Legislature can
remedy some of the evils complained of, and your attention
is earnestly invited to the subject, in order that whatever is
practicable may be done to guard the purity of the ballot-box,
and the rights of electors.   .

WRITS OF ERROR IN CIMINAL CASES.

The attention of the Legislature is again invited to the importance of writs of error in criminal cases, and reference is
made to my last two annual messages for the arguments and
reasons why there should be additional legislation upon this
subject.

EDUCATION.

With great propriety, the Superintendent, in the opening
of his able report, congratulates the people upon the continued growth and prosperity of our public schools.

Their progress is clearly indicated by comparing the expenditures of the last six years, with those of the six years
prior to 1867, viz :

Total cost for tuition from 1867 to 1872............	$21,578,258 61
Total cost for tuition from 1861 to 1866...........	12,745,061 71
Increase.............	$8,833,196 90
Total expenditures of the system from 1867 to 1872,	$42,952,152 11
Total expenditures of the system from 1861 to 1866,	19,590,149 51
Increase.......	$23,361,902 60

Pennsylvania, less fortunate than many of her sister States,
has no school fund. The legislative appropriations amount
only to about six hundred thousand dollars annually; but

the people, in the several districts, voluntarily vote all other moneys necessary to support the schools. The foregoing statements briefly exhibit the deep and increasing interest entertained in behalf of popular education.

Intelligence and virtue are conceded to be indispensable conditions of the permament existence and prosperity of any form of government. The necessity of these supports increases in proportion as the area of freedom and privilege is enlarged. It follows, from these unquestioned maxims, that the demand for general education is more imperative in the United States than in any other country. Our Constitution recognizes the people as the inherent source of all power. All participate in the great act of creating the country's rulers. The ballot decides all questions of choice, and fills all official positions, from that of the chief magistrate of the nation to that of the lowest town officer. This supreme and resistless power of universal suffrage, at once suggests the absolute necessity of universal education. The truth of these premises admitted, no argument is required to establish the conclusion.

The common school system doubtless owes its origin to a common conviction that no people can be properly and permanently self-governing, whose intelligence is unequal to the comprehension of their rights, privileges and responsibilities, or whose virtues are too feeble and imperfect to restrain them from a violation of those duties which they owe to their Creator and to each other.

When the system was introduced, thirty-eight years ago, it was generally viewed in the light of an experiment. The act creating it made its adoption dependent upon the vote of the people in their respective districts. Their reluctant and tardy acceptance of the priceless boon is neither matter of surprise to us, nor reproach to them, when all the circumstances are duly considered. Its present popularity is indicated by the entire absence of complaint, and a still more significant readiness, by the people, to assume the expenses requisite for its constant improvement and efficient application. Doubtless many years must elapse before the full fruition of its influences can be received, but, meanwhile, it will be gradually moulding the popular mind into more perfect conformity with the requirements of our free institutions.

Fortunately the old *prejudice* against the system no longer exists; but *indifference*, to a lamentable extent, occupies its place. From the report of the Superintendent it appears that the number of children in the State, who do not attend school, exceeds seventy-five thousand. This criminal neglect is most prevalent in the cities. In Philadelphia twelve per cent. of the children between the ages of five and fifteen years do not attend school. But more significant and alarming still, of the whole number registered as attendants, forty-six per cent. are absent from the daily sessions. In the State at large the unregistered amount to six per cent., and the absentees to thirty-three per cent. And, as was naturally to be expected, the resulting ignorance from this neglect has proved a fruitful source of crime. Sixteen per cent. of the inmates of the State prisons are unable to read.

Obviously, therefore, it is not sufficient that the State makes ample provision. Such measures should be immediately adopted as would secure a universal participation of the benefit. The children are not to blame. They naturally prefer freedom and amusement to the confinement and studies of the school room. Parents and guardians are the parties with whom the State must deal. She owes it alike to her own peace and security, and to the highest welfare of the children who are to be her future citizens, to see that they shall be rescued from the perils of ignorance.

After careful and anxious deliberation upon all the facts, and their inevitable consequences, I recommend the adoption of a *compulsory system* of education. That a law to this effect will encounter objections is not to be doubted; fr ino view of the probability of such a measure, its opponents have already commenced to marshal their forces.

In Norway, Sweden and Prussia this system was first adopted, and such have been its salutary effects that other European governments have made haste to follow their example. Austria, admonished by the defeat at Sadowa, France by the crushing disaster at Sedan, and England by the possibility of a real "battle of Dorking," have decreed by statute that all their children shall be taught to read and write, influenced by a conviction that knowledge gives increased prowess in war as well as capacity and integrity for the peaceful pursuits of life. And it is a fact of striking significance that none of the States that have passed such enactments have abandoned or repealed them.

In passing from this topic, of paramount importance to the future well-being of the Commonwealth, I unhesitatingly express the hope that the day is not distant when through the Bureau of National Education, seconded by the concurrent legislative action of the States, every child in the American Union, without reference to creed, caste, color or condition, will be thoroughly and effectually instructed in all the elementary branches of English education ; and that uniform text books, setting forth the true history and theory of our National and State governments, will be provided and introduced into all the schools of the country. Approximation of thought and opinion on these subjects is of vital consequence to the permanence of the Union, and the stability of our republican institutions. Had such a measure been opportunely initiated the war of the rebellion would scarcely have been possible.

Should you deem your powers inadequate to enact suitable laws upon this subject, the Constitutional Convention, now in session, should not hesitate to habilitate you with such authority, and thus lend their aid and influence in making

Pennsylvania the vanguard in the great mission of universal education.

From the report of the Superintendent of Soldiers' Orphans' schools, and other sources, I feel fully authorized in assuring you they were never before in a more flourishing and prosperous condition.

Every child, legally eligible, and having made application, is now admitted to these schools. The whole number of admissions since 1865 is 6,429; the discharges from all causes 2,902, leaving in attendance 3,527. No larger number will probably hereafter be attained, and it may confidently be expected that this number will be subject to an annual reduction of at least 500, until the system shall have accomplished its mission.

The entire expense of these schools to the State, since they went into operation in 1865, is $3,467,543 11. Their cost during the last year was $475,245 47. It is estimated by the Superintendent that the future expense, to the period of their final extinction, will not exceed one million five hundred thousand dollars.

The health of the children has been excellent. Their exemption from small-pox, while it was prevailing all around them, is remarkable; and no stronger evidence of good management and the propitious results of systematic vaccination, could be adduced. The exemplary conduct of the pupils after their discharge is one of the most gratifying circumstances connected with their history. The following statement of the Superintendent will be highly satisfactory to the Legislature and the people: "From the beginning of these schools to the present, the greater part of the children who have received their advantages have been honorably discharged. And from facts in the possession of the department, it appears that *more than ninety-eight per cent. are doing well, and seem likely to become upright and useful citizens.*"

Among the States of the American Union, Pennsylvania stands pre-eminent in her "care for the soldier who has borne the battle, and for his widow and orphan children." Her noble scheme for clothing, educating, maintaining and adopting the orphan children of her soldiers who gave their lives in defense of the National Union, is her own invention. In this the generosity of her people has been imitated, but not equalled by those of any other State. To her will forever be accorded the leadership in this work of patriotic benevolence. It will form the brightest page of her history. It will seal the devotion of her people to the common country; and our legislators, in view of its benign influences, will continue to accord a cheerful and liberal support to a system so fruitful in blessing to the orphan children of our martyred heroes.

Upon no material interest of the State is the influence of education more salutory than that of agriculture. Pennsylvania, by wise legislation, has authorized the purchase of three experimental farms, and the establishment of a college, all of which are now in successful operation, and the results of the scientific working of the farms have already added much practical knowledge upon the general subject.

The Agricultural College has just closed a most prosperous year—the number of students being one hundred and fifty—which exceeds that of any year since the opening of the institution. Any one, of three courses, is optional to the students, viz: Agricultural, scientific or classical, to all of which is added a general course of military instruction.

The admission of females, which was first permitted sixteen months ago, has thus far worked exceedingly well. Thirty young women have availed themselves of the opportunity thus afforded to obtain a first-class education.

All students are taught to regard labor as beneficial and honorable. The rule of the college requiring ten hours manual labor per week from the students is cheerfully complied with, and results advantageously to their health and comfort.

This State institution is pre-eminently the *People's College.* Its preparatory department receives students at a low grade, as well as those more advanced. This school is "cheap enough for the poorest and good enough for the richest," either in mind or estate; and it affords healthful exercise, instruction 'in useful labor, and free tuition in every branch of its ample courses of study.

THE NATIONAL GUARD.

For the details of the organization of the National Guard, and the general business of the Adjutant General's Department, your attention is invited to the accompanying report of that officer.

At the close of the late war the State was without a single military division, and the few scattered companies which existed at its commencement had been, generally, disbanded by the enlistment of their members in the active military service of the General Government.

In 1866 the militia of the State comprised only eight volunteer companies. Since then four hundred and eighty-three have been organized and one hundred and sixty-eight disbanded—the latter principally on account of the almost entire want of encouragement and support from the State, and their own inability to maintain themselves. To this fact is mainly attributable the reduction of the volunteer force in the First division (Philadelphia) during the past year. The Legislature, at its last session, having repealed all laws by which any military fund could be raised in that division, left its organizations entirely dependent upon themselves and the voluntary contributions of citizens.

The organizations of the National Guard, *not yet disbanded,* consist of fifteen regiments and six battalions; comprising, with unattached bodies, three hundred and twenty-three companies, viz: Six artillery, eight cavalry, and three hun-died and nine infantry. The aggregate of enlisted men is 13,565, and of commissioned officers 1,126.

Convinced of the necessity, in time of peace as well as in war, of an efficient military force to maintain the civil authority, I have at all times entertained a deep interest in the military department of the State, and it affords me pleasure to say that the present condition of our volunteer organizations is as complete as is practicable under the admitted imperfections and illiberal provisions of our military laws.

Where "the greater security of life and property" is the question involved, it would seem superfluous to employ arguments to convince any property holder, business man, or good citizen, that it was his *individual interest* to support a system designed to uphold the civil authority. But as practical illustrations, of recent date, I may refer to the scenes of July, 1871, in the city of New York, as well as to those enacted in our own State, at Scranton, during the months of April and May, of the same year, and still more recently followed by the disturbance of the public peace in July last, which so seriously threatened the city of Williamsport. The civil arm of the law was paralyzed, and peaceable citizens were at the mercy of the rioters. Appeals came from the civil authorities and the people, for the protection of the military against tumult which they were unable to quell. The military of the nearest divisions promptly responded to the call of the Executive, the majesty of the civil law was vindicated in the suppression of the disorder, and at comparatively trifling cost to the State, the peace and quiet of two of her flourishing cities were restored, immensely valuable property preserved, and very many honest and industrious laborers enabled to resume the work on which the subsistence of themselves and their families depended. Such occurrences surely demonstrate both the value and necessity of a well organized and thoroughly disciplined National Guard to maintain the civil authority. I cite these circumstances as an act of official duty, and from a desire to avail myself of this opportunity of leaving on record my appreciation of the importance of such action, on your part, as will maintain a well equipped, disciplined and reliable State military force.

For a full statement of the disturbances at Williamsport, and of the operations of the military called into service, on appeal of the civil authorities, you are referred to the official statement of Major General Jesse Merrill, commanding the 11th Division, which appears at length in the Adjutant General's report.

The discreet and judicious conduct of the Major General, and the officers and men under his command on that occasion, not only won the approval of the citizens of that community, but entitles them to general commendation.

Provision should be promptly made for the payment of the expenses necessarily incurred on pay rolls and accounts duly audited and certified by the proper officers; the amount of which will not exceed fifteen thousand dollars.

PICTURE OF THE BATTLE OF GETTYSBURG.

The period determined upon by the Legislature for the delivery of the picture of the battle of Gettysburg, painted for the State by P. F. Rothermel, artist, having arrived, no place in the Capitol, or other public buildings at Harrisburg, was found suitable for its reception and exhibition. Finding that the picture could not long remain rolled up without considerable injury, and, perhaps, total destruction; with the approval of several members of the Senate and of the House, I consented to place it in the hands of the Park Commissioners of Philadelphia, subject to the order of the Legislature.

A building 140 feet long and 43 feet wide has been erected in Fairmount Park for the reception of this historic painting, within a few hundred feet of the Green street entrance. The site is the very best that could have been selected to afford the public easy access. The gallery is perfectly adapted for the safe keeping and proper exhibition of the picture.

RECORDING DOCUMENTS AND BINDING LAW BOOKS.

Under existing laws many important documents are filed in the office of the Secretary of the Commonwealth, which, for greater security, ought to be recorded in suitable books for that purpose. Prominent among those referred to may be enumerated papers relating to the merger and consolidation of railroad companies; the increase of capital stock and bonded obligations of corporations under both general and special laws; correction of errors, and confirming corporate organizations; extension of charters and dissolution of corporations; the change of name of corporations and the location of their principal offices; the acceptance of the provisions of acts of Assembly by corporations; and contracts to which the State is a party. This list might be extended, but enough has been given to indicate the grave importance of the interests involved, and the necessity for the utmost care in preserving, in proper and accessible shape, the evidence of such transactions. I therefore recommend such enactments as will confer the authority required upon the Secretary of the Commonwealth.

The State authorizes the publication of the statute laws, and the distribution of them to sundry enumerated officers and persons. Justices of the peace and aldermen are required to carefully preserve the copies received by them and hand them over to their successors in office. But the annual volumes being large, and bound only in paper covers, it is almost impossible to preserve them whole for any reasonable time. I recommend the passage of a law requiring them to be properly bound before distribution.

BOARD OF PUBLIC CHARITIES.

.The eminent and philanthropic gentlemen composing the Board of Public Charities have carefully investigated a number of subjects which they deemed of sufficient importance to lay before the Legislature. Among them may be specially noticed Prison Discipline,—a question now generally occupying the attention of statesmen and philanthropists throughout the civilized world; the condition and treatment of the insane and the workings of that class of institutions known as local charities, founded and conducted for benevolent purposes. These asylums are located in various parts of the State, mostly, however, in Philadelphia and Pittsburg. They are performing an excellent work—relieving the sick, indigent, infirm and neglected portions of our population. The General Agent has devoted a considerable portion of his time to their inspection, the results of which will appear in his able report to the Board, in which he exhibits their character and the large amount of private charity bestowed upon them.

This Board was organized during my administration, and I have entertained a deep and lasting interest in its labors. The gentlemen who compose it voluntarily devote their time, without compensation, to this noble work of benevolence. The impress of their intelligent efforts is every where perceptible; and the large annual contributions of the State to charitable institutions have, under their supervision and examination, been properly and systematically applied.

The third volume of their reports will be submitted at an early day. It will present a large amount of statistical information, and many interesting facts and valuable suggestions upon subjects of great importance. I cannot too strongly commend this Board—the great regulator of State charities—to the favorable consideration of the Legislature, and recommend such appropriations for expenses and additional enactments as may be necessary to increase its efficiency.

PENITENTIARIES AND REFORMATORIES.

From a personal inspection of the penitentiaries, I am able to bear testimony to the evidences that were everywhere manifested of their general good management and excellent discipline.

The Eastern penitentiary has long been deservedly regarded as the model prison in which the "separate" or "individual treatment" system of imprisonment is applied, and the annual reports of its faithful Board of Inspectors, embracing their observations and investigations, show that they have elevated the subject of crime-punishment almost to the dignity of a science.

Among the circumstances that attracted my attention was the insufficient number of cells to carry out the "solitary confinement" principle, and the incarceration there of a number of boys and youths for first offences, and of females untrained in crime. Sometimes two or more in one cell were thus unavoidably brought into associations which could scarcely fail to produce contamination of character and morals. I would, therefore, recommend that the Legislature enable the courts to sentence minors and females to the county prisons, where with proper teaching—training in some handy-craft business—and with due attention given to discipline, the object of punishment would be more effectually attained; and the penitentiary, thus relieved, would have cells sufficient for all ordinary purposes. It is a great mistake in almost all cases of minors convicted for their first, and often trivial offence, to send them to a State's prison; because the punishment is less in its effect than the idea of degradation in the after-life of the prisoner. Such persons should be punished in the locality where the crime was committed, and the disgrace would not be so likely to permanently affect the character after the discharge of the prisoner.

From 1829 to 1871, inclusive, only three hundred and forty-six females were received in the Eastern penitentiary, and of this number one hundred and twenty-seven were minors. These facts would fully justify the propriety of such action by the Legislature as has been suggested.

The Western penitentiary contains ample space for present demands. It is conducted on the "combined" system of "solitary" and "congregate" imprisonment, the workings of which are giving entire satisfaction to all concerned.

The commissioners from this State to the International Prison Congress, lately held in London, England, report that twenty-one governments were represented, principally by men who have made criminal legislation and penal treatment a study. America sent seventy-three delegates, representing penitentiaries, asylums and reformatory institutions. Among these were many experts in every branch of penology. The deliberations of the Congress continued ten days. Its results are difficult to estimate; but it is hoped the great interests of humanity involved in the proper treatment of crime will be happily subserved among all civilized nations.

The managers of the "Pennsylvania Reform School" (late the Western House of Refuge) propose to change their location from Allegheny City to a farm, containing 503 acres, in Washington county, seventeen miles from Pittsburg, near the Chartiers Valley railroad, and adopt for its government the best features of what is known as the "family system" of juvenile reformatories. These will mainly consist in the abandonment of walls, bolts and bars for confining the children; and in an earnest effort govern them through sympathy and kindness, and prepare them for useful occupations.

The Board will ask an additional appropriation to pay for the land and improvements.

SANITARY REGULATIONS.

Of all my official recommendations, I deem those most important which relate to the public health. Facilities for the material development, and the accumulation of wealth,

estimated at their highest value, are of but minor consequence
when compared with the preservation of life itself. "All that
a man hath will he give for his life!" At the time of pre-
senting my last annual message, small-pox was fearfully
prevalent in Philadelphia and in many towns and populous
districts of the State. I then called attention to the subject,
and in the strongest terms at my command, urged the imperative necessity of adopting such measures as would arrest
the disease and prevent its re-appearance. My suggestions,
however, were utterly unheeded by the Legislature. The
dreadful scourge extended itself into the first half of the past
year, and, in the absence of well known preventives, it would
be presumption not to expect its annual return. Neither the
extent of its ravages, nor the fatal character of the disease,
last year, is generally known to the public, or, I am confident, there would have been such an outcry as would have
compelled immediate attention and relief. Among the un-
vaccinated, the ordinary proportion of deaths has been thirty-
three per cent.; but the recent death-rate in Philadelphia
amounted to nearly forty-seven per cent. This is fearful
to contemplate, and yet, more fearful still—the fatal per-
centage has been nearly sixty-six in the country at large.
This is mainly the result of an indifference, so reckless, as to
be absolutely unaccountable. I am thoroughly convinced,
that the deplorable results now alluded to, might have been
prevented, by opportune legislation. The testimony of the
most scientific schools is to the effect that vaccination, properly administered, is a sovereign antidote. The highest
medical authorities unqualifiedly affirm small-pox to be a
disgrace to any civilized land; that there is no necessity for
its presence, and that if every person were properly vaccinated every seven years, the disease might be utterly exter-
minated. I am assured of the correctness of this opinion by
my personal observations in the army, both in Mexico and
the United States. Soon after our camps were pitched upon

Mexican soil, the disease made its appearance among our troops. By an order from General Scott, the whole army was immediately vaccinated, and the small-pox was at once driven from our lines. The same result followed the application of the same remedy in the army of General Sherman, during his famous march "to the sea," and, more recently, in our very midst we have been favored with an illustration equally striking and conclusive: Our schools of soldiers' orphans, in which there are upwards of thirty-five hundred children, being under the absolute control of the State authorities, a regulation enforcing universal vaccination, could be, and was, adopted. The result is, that not a single case of small-pox has occurred in them.

My object in submitting these remarks to you is not so much for the purpose of convincing you of the truth of a proposition which but few attempt to dispute, as to ask the immediate enactment of remedial measures. It remains, therefore, only to consider how the object to be sought may be most speedily and effectually accomplished. In reply to this question, I earnestly recommend the passage of an act providing for *compulsory* vaccination, which should have such penalties annexed as would insure its undoubted enforcement.

I also recommend an enactment establishing a State Board of Health, whose functions shall be discharged under the auspices of the Legislature. Such an organization would be indispensable to the vigorous and comprehensive execution of a law making vaccination compulsory, and would be eminently serviceable in enforcing such other sanitary regulations as might be deemed essential to the protection of the public against small-pox and other contagious diseases. The State Board might be constituted somewhat upon the model of the Board of Public Charities, with the addition of local boards for the counties, cities and larger towns. The expense of such a system would not be worth a thought, when compared with the value of the benefits that would be conferred.

3

by its operation. At all events, it would be far less than the cost in human lives annually sacrificed by the diseases it would be designed to prevent. It is not possible to estimate correctly such values. But for the purpose of illustration, the calculation of an eminent physician may be accepted. Dr. Ackland, of England, sets down every death by a preventable disease as a loss in money of £100, and £12 for loss of time and maintenance during the period of sickness. According to this standard Pennsylvania lost during the last two years by small-pox alone more than $5,000,000.

From a joint report made to me by the Health Officer and Port Physician of Philadelphia, I learn that the health laws of that city and port are in a very confused and unsatisfactory condition. These gentlemen, in effect, say that the first comprehensive health law was passed in 1818; that continuous additions have been made since that time; that while some of the laws have been repealed, others have became inoperative and obsolete; that if certain of these were revived and enforced their execution would inflict positive injury, and, in short, that the whole system imperatively requires a thorough revision. I have good reason to endorse the truth of these statements, and I earnestly recommend the whole subject to your early and considerate action, and that the amendments which you may make for the better protection of the health and general well-being of Philadelphia be extended as far as practicable to the whole State.

CAPITOL AND CAPITOL GROUNDS.

The apartment in the Capitol building, familiarly known as the "Office of the State Historian," has been tastefully fitted up for the reception and display of the battle-flags carried by our soldiers in the war of the rebellion, in accordance with a resolution to that effect passed by the Legislature at its last session.

For the purpose of irrigating and beautifying the Capitol grounds, I recommend that you authorize the construction of at least two ornamental fountains.

I renew my recommendation for the purchase of a few small lots at the eastern corner of the grounds necessary to the completion of the square, and that the iron fence enclosing them be completed.

GOVERNOR'S SALARY.

As no charge of selfishness can, at this juncture, attach to me, I frankly remind you that the compensation of the Governor is entirely inadequate to enable him to live in a style corresponding to his position, and the reasonable expectations of the people of so great a Commonwealth. The truth of these assertions is so obvious that no argument is required for their confirmation.

The Constitution declares in section VI, of article II, "The Governor shall, at stated times, receive for his services a compensation, which shall be neither increased nor diminished during the period for which he shall have been elected."

Should the Legislature concur with me as to the propriety of increasing the compensation of the Executive to ten thousand dollars per annum, I recommend that it be done prior to the twentieth of January, as on that day the period for which my successor has been elected will begin.

IN MEMORIAM.

It has heretofore been my sad duty to chronicle the departure of distinguished citizens from spheres of usefulness to that realm of eternal silence, from which no traveler returns. Among them may be enumerated three ex-Governors; and now I am called upon to announce the decease of another who has occupied the Executive chair.

WILLIAM F. JOHNSTON was born November 29, 1808, at Greensburg, Westmoreland county, and died at Pittsburg, October 25, 1872, in the sixty-fourth year of his age.

He was admitted to the bar in 1829, and was subsequently a member of the House of Representatives, and of the Senate. As speaker of the latter, he became acting Governor upon the resignation of Francis R. Shunk. He was afterwards nominated by the Whigs, and elected to the Chief Magistracy. He filled the office with honor and marked ability. After the expiration of his term he devoted his time to the construction and management of railroads and the development of the resources of the western portion of the State. He was endowed with strong natural abilities, was genial in manners and faithful in friendship. His services to the Commonwealth will not soon be forgotten. I trust the Legislature will do justice to his memory by appropriately noticing his death.

It is with profound sorrow, also, that I announce to you, officially, the death of Major General GEORGE GORDON MEADE. He died in Philadelphia, November 6, 1872, in the fifty-sixth year of his age.

It is impossible, within the brief space allowed, to give an extended notice of the services of one so eminently distinguished. He was a graduate of the Military Academy at West Point; and served with distinction in the Seminole and Mexican wars, and as a Topographical Engineer in time of peace. At the commencement of the recent Civil war, his services were tendered to and accepted by the Government. From the rank of Brigadier General he rose through the grades of Division and Corps Commander, and was on the twenty-eighth day of June, 1863, without solicitation, appointed, by President Lincoln, Commander-in-Chief of the Army of the Potomac; and although he leaves behind him an undying record of his brilliant and heroic deeds wherever he was called into action, his name will be, particularly and forever, associated with the glory of the great turning battle of the war—fought at Gettysburg, on the first, second and third days of July, 1863.

General Meade remained in the regular army until the time of his death. He was an accomplished gentleman, possessing a highly cultivated intellect, sound judgment, and great integrity of character. But it is to his distinguished services upon the soil of Pennsylvania, which has so intimately identified his memory with the defence of the nation, in the hour of its extremest peril, that I invoke your special attention. Pennsylvania *cannot, will not* be ungrateful for such services. She will desire, with appropriate honors, to perpetuate the fame of her departed chieftain. I recommend an appropriation for the erection of a monument to his memory upon the battle-field of Gettysburg; and such other legislation as will be alike suitable to the occasion and honorable to the Commonwealth.

PARDONS, COMMUTATIONS AND EXECUTIONS.

No department of the State government has imposed upon it such difficult and embarrassing duties, or such weighty and disagreeable responsibilities, as the pardoning power devolves upon the Executive.

That a few pardons may have been unworthily granted, through the misrepresentations of relatives, neighbors, or other *interested* parties, or even by *affidavits* afterwards discovered to have been designedly false, may be frankly conceded; and that some who, perhaps, were more deserving, have been refused, from want of proper representations of facts, may be equally true; still, I feel assured that I have faithfully performed my duty in such cases, and have exercised the prerogative only when the facts and circumstances seemed to imperatively demand the interposition of Executive clemency. In this, I have endeavored to adopt and enforce the views entertained by the framers of our Constitution, who never contemplated an indiscriminate use of the pardoning power, but designed it for the correction of errors and oppressions; cases of after discovered evidence; inequalities of sentences for identical offences; the furtherance of justice by uncovering crime, and other instances strongly exceptional in their character.

Soon after entering upon the duties of the Executive office, I deemed it important that the public should be more fully informed upon the subject of pardons, than they had previously been. I then introduced, for the first time in this State, an annual pardon report, containing the names of the petitioners, and an epitome of the reasons adduced for each case of relief from the sentence of the law. Since then, similar reports have been made in other States, and the practice, divesting the exercise of the pardoning prerogative of all secrecy, seems to have received very general approbation

The applications for pardons, during the past year, numbered one thousand four hundred and thirty-seven—about five for every working day in the year. Of these, sixty-nine were granted—less than five per cent. of the number applied for, and averaging about one to each county. Estimating our population at three million six hundred thousand, the average is one pardon to every forty-two thousand three hundred.

The system of commutation, under the act of May 21, 1869, continues to work well in all the prisons, and has produced a decidedly salutary effect upon the discipline of the prisons and the character of the prisoners.

The death penalty has been twice carried into effect during the year, once in Cambria county and once in Chester.

A report of pardons and executions for the year ending November 30, 1872, accompanies this communication.

IMPROVEMENT OF THE OHIO RIVER.

The subject of the improvement of the Ohio river and its navigable tributaries has long engaged the attention of leading business men of our own and other States, and they have several times solicited Congressional action in its behalf. Organized effort was commenced during the present year. A convention met in Cincinnati on the twentieth of last February, in which a comparison of views led to the adoption of a resolution requesting the Governors of the States of Pennsylvania, West Virginia, Indiana, Illinois, Ohio, Kentucky and Tennessee, to appoint each a committee of five members, who should act as a commission to take charge of, and promote by all legitimate means the desired improvement. I responded to the request, and appointed as commissioners for Pennsylvania, James K. Moorhead, Thomas J. Powers, George H. Thurston, Joseph Walton and Edward Blanchard. The Governors of the other States made similar appointments, and the commission met at Cincinnati on the eighteenth of September. It continued in session two days, and its proceedings indicate that its members were actuated by earnestness of spirit, and by just, comprehensive and statesmanlike views.

The commission from its own body appointed committees on statistics, legislation, water supply and available reservoirs, plans and manner of improvement, and an executive committee, with power to act in the intervals of its regular sessions. Resolutions were adopted asking the Governors of the several States represented, to present the subject upon which the commission had been created in their forthcoming messages to their respective Legislatures—to advise them to instruct their Senators and request their Representatives in Congress to favor a liberal policy toward an interest of such magnitude, and to recommend them to make an appropriation sufficient to pay the expenses of the commission.

From a memorial prepared and submitted to the commission by Mr. Thurston, it is manifest that the project is one of the very highest importance to the States immediately concerned, and indirectly of great interest to the whole country. The claims of this subject to your prompt and favorable consideration, and that of Congress will hardly be questioned, when it is remembered that it is presented by gentlemen who represent one-half of the population of the country; that the people, who would be directly or indirectly benefited by the contemplated improvement, possess one-half of its cultivated lands, raise sixty per cent. of its agricultural products, breed sixty per cent. of its live stock, own fifty per cent. of its capital invested in farming implements and machinery, and have, heretofore, paid thirty-five per cent. of its internal taxation, and contributed a corresponding share toward the payment of the National debt.

The President of the United States, in his late message, invites the attention of Congress to this and similar enterprises, as being of great moment to the varied producing intersts and the internal commerce of the country in time of peace, " and of inestimable value in case of a foreign war." In the scheme for the improvement of the Ohio river and its navigable tributaries, Pennsylvania has an immediate and deep concern. The subject, as presented by Mr. Thurston, has awakened in my own mind an unreserved and ardent sympathy, and I refer you with pleasure to his very comprehensive and able report, and most cordially recommend that the instructions requested, and an appropriation to meet the necessary expenses of our commissioners, be given. I am informed that the amount required by the commissioners of each State will not exceed three thousand dollars. It need scarcely be added that the character of the gentlemen composing the commission entitles them to your perfect confidence, and gives assurance that the appropriation would be judiciously and honestly expended.

CENTENNIAL.

On the fourth of July, 1876, the nation will have completed the first century of its existence. The design to celebrate that great event in a becoming manner doubtless commends itself alike to your intelligent appreciation of the blessings of liberty and independence, and your highest sentiments of patriotic pride and gratitude. Already the preliminary steps of the design have been taken, and toward its happy realization the people of the entire country are looking with profound interest and pleasure. By a combination of circumstances, well known in history, in the metropolis of our State the Declaration of Independence was proclaimed, and the Constitution subsequently adopted.

That city has, therefore, very naturally been selected as the scene of the proposed Centennial Celebration and International Exhibition.

A popular manifestation of this kind should correspond to the character of the event to be celebrated. It will be the first Centennial celebration of our national existence—the greatest event that can possibly occur in the life-time of any living American; it will be the first international exhibition ever given in honor of Republican Government, and will exhibit the effect of our institutions in promoting wealth, intelligence and happiness. The ceremonies of this unprecedented occasion should be noted for spontaneous enthusiasm, universal enlistment of popular sentiment, and a more impressive grandeur than has ever heretofore been witnessed.

The enterprise, which cannot fail to interest the whole country, must prove unusually attractive to Philadelphians, and scarcely less so to the whole people of the Commonwealth; and it is certainly to be expected that they will be peculiarly distinguished for earnestness and zeal in its support. The city having thus far borne all the expenses attending the organization and meetings of the United States Com-

missioners, and having extended to them graceful courtesies
and liberal hospitality, it may be well now to consider what
the State may do to advance the cause, and what further
action or aid in the premises may be expected from the General Government.

Naturally desiring to have no financial trusts in this connection, and feeling the need of an executive arm capable of
performing the many business functions essential to the success of the undertaking, the National Commissioners asked
Congress to authorize the organization of a corporation,
under the title of the "Centennial Board of Finance," with a
capital stock amounting to ten million dollars, divided into
shares of ten dollars each, with the power of acquiring and
holding such real and personal estate as may be needed in
carrying into effect the act of Congress, approved March 3,
1871.

An act embodying these privileges was promptly passed
by Congress, June 1, 1871, and under it books for the subscription of the stock have been opened in each State and
Territory, and the organization of the Board of Finance will
probably be completed before the adjournment of the Legislature.

The quota of stock allotted to Pennsylvania will be
promptly taken, and more than this its people cannot do,
until the hundred days, prior to the organization of the Board
of Finance, in which the subscription books are required to
be kept open in each State and Territory, shall have elapsed;
after which time, any stock not taken, should, if not called
for by others, be promptly subscribed by our citizens.

Under the eleventh article of the Constitution, the State is
prohibited from subscribing for stocks or lending its credit
for any other object than the payment of its own debt, or for
the purpose of military defence. But it can and should make
such a special donation as would inspire popular confidence,
excite the emulation of other States, and insure the prompt

commencement of the work upon a scale commensurate with
its importance.

The eighth section of the original act of Congress authorizing the exhibition, provides "that whenever the President
shall be informed by the Governor of the State of Pennsylvania that provision has been made for the erection of suitable buildings for the purpose, and for the exclusive control by
the commission herein provided for, of the proposed exposi-
tion, the President shall, through the Department of State,
make proclamation of the same, setting forth the time at
which the exhibition will open and the place at which it shall
be held; and he shall communicate to the diplomatic representatives of all nations copies of the same, together with
such regulations as may be adopted by the commissioners,
for publication in their respective countries."

The provisions authorizing the organization of the Board
of Finance, and the formal proclamation of the national and
international character of the exhibition is deferred until the
the Governor of this Commonwealth can make the required
report to the President of the United States. I would, therefore, recommend to your honorable bodies to make a sufficient appropriation for the purpose of securing the erection ·
of suitable buildings for holding the exhibition, to be under
the cotrol of the National Commission in accordance with the
act of Congress.

I would further recommend that your "Committee on Fed-.
eral Relations" consider the propriety of asking Congress to
make an appropriation for such necessary expenses of the
National Commissioners as will enable them to work with
efficiency. The members are national officers charged with
a trust of great responsibility, and engaged in an enterprise
in which the reputation of the country is directly involved.

Our Government, which expended a large sum of money
in promoting the Paris exhibition, certainly will not treat the
agents to whom it has committed the task of preparing a

memorial of its birth upon its own soil, in the form of an International Exhibition of the Arts of Modern Civilization, with such parsimony as would deprive them of their proper influence, dignity and independence.

The State Commissioners heretofore appointed under the acts of the Legislature have made no report of their transactions, and may not yet have found their proper sphere of usefulness. They can render much service to the United States Commissioners, and to the Board of Finance, by obtaining subscriptions of stock, and promoting such organization of the industries of the State as would contribute to the success of the exhibition, and present an appropriate display of the wealth and resources of the Commonwealth.

This great national enterprise appeals as well to local pride as to common patriotism; it must be successful—the nation has decreed it; and since to Pennsylvania has been assigned the honor of having the celebration take place on her soil, she must and will see to it that it shall not fail. I, therefore, earnestly solicit for it not only your aid but also the thoughtful and zealous support of all social, industrial, scientific, educational and religious associations, and that of all good citizens, who have at heart the honor, perpetuity, and happiness of our common country.

GENERAL REMARKS.

In my official communications, heretofore, to the Legislature, and in public addresses to the people, I have without hesitation declared my views in favor of protection to our Home Industries, and in defence of labor against foreign competition. Continued observation and experience have tended to confirm me as to the correctness of the opinions then expressed. I now reiterate them with undiminished confidence; and feel peculiar satisfaction in the belief that Congress will maintain a policy that has so vastly contributed to the prosperity of the whole country.

The inter-state courtecies, heretofore exercised, have been continued and fostered by a system of mutual exchanges of the laws and other public documents; and in the enforcement of statutes authorizing requisitions, and the rendition of fugitive criminals. During my administration there has not occurred a single circumstance to mar the harmony and friendship existing between the Government of Pennsylvania and that of any other State, or of the Nation. The obvious advantages arising from such a condition of our affairs must naturally tend to advance the best interests of the States, and cement the bonds of the National Union.

The recent elections prove, by unprecedented majorities, that the country reposes extraordinary confidence in the patriotism, sagacity and integrity of the Republican party. In response to this sentiment, that party should discharge its sacred trust by a wise, honest, economical and patriotic administration of the government; a thorough reform of the civil service; the continuation of such duties upon foreign imports as will secure and enhance the prosperity of our domestic manufactures; the reduction of the scale of internal taxes to the lowest degree that would be adequate to the maintenance of the public credit and the gradual extinction of the national debt; the restoration of our foreign commerce; the extension of ample financial facilities for the requirements of business; the encouragement and regulation of immigration; the increase of the means of cheap land and water transportation, with a view to the largest and most rapid development of the national resources; and such enforcement of the provisions of the amended Constitution as will preserve peace in the States and secure, beyond the touch of injustice and oppression, the rights of all citizens.

All the circumstances considered, I may, in this connection be excused for the indulgence of some brief personal allusions. In the administration of the Chief Magistracy, I have, with only good intentions, and unconscious of intentional error, to the best of my ability, endeavored to discharge the various duties that have devolved upon me, in such manner as to advance the public welfare, by condemning waste and extravagance, practicing economy, reducing taxation, paying the State debt, promoting the public health, advancing the cause of general education, cultivating humanity and charity, tempering justice from the fountain of mercy, maintaining the principles of the Constitution, and defending the honor and sovereignty of the State, and the rights and interests of her citizens.

During my administration the Legislature has been in session three hundred and eighty-seven days; in that time nine thousand two hundred and forty-two bills, and one hundred and fourteen resolutions, were passed, of which eight thousand eight hundred and forty-two bills, and one hundred and thirteen resolutions, received my approval; six became laws without my sanction, and three hundred and ninety were vetoed. The vetoes average a little more than one per diem during the sessions, and all of which, with the exception of four, were sustained by the Legislature. In addition to my six annual messages, I have also transmitted to the Legislature one hundred and five special communications.

The period for disconnecting my official relations with the General Assembly having almost arrived, I may properly avail myself of this opportunity to acknowledge the general courtesy I have received from the successive Legislatures with whom I have had the honor to hold official intercourse, and to express the profound sense of gratitude I entertain toward the people of my native State, for the many honors they have conferred upon me, and still more for the steadfast confidence with which they have supported me, and sustained my administration.

To Hon. Francis Jordan, Secretary of State; Hon. Frederick Carroll Brewster, Attorney General; Hon. James P. Wickersham, Superintendent of Schools, and General Alexander Russell, Adjutant General, I tender my warmest and special thanks, for their hearty accord and energetic support. I owe them not only a debt of gratitude for their personal fidelity, but a sincere and heart-felt commendation to the people, for the able, efficient and eminently satisfactory manner in which they have performed all the duties that have been devolved upon them in their several departments. Col. Benjamin F. Lee, my Private Secretary, and his assistant, Col. William C. Armor, are deserving of honorable mention, for their zealous and faithful execution of my orders. My thanks are also due, and they are earnestly tendered, to the clerks and other appointees in the several departments, for their uniform courtesy, and the zeal manifested by them for the public good.

It affords me peculiar satisfaction to feel that my official honors and responsibilities are shortly to be transferred into the hands of a gentleman, who will sacredly guard the one, and faithfully discharge the other. Major General John F. Hartranft has signally illustrated his courage and patriotism on many fiercely contested fields of battle; and qualities, that have made his reputation as a soldier, have been no less conspicuous in the pursuits of civil life. He will bring to the discharge of his duties a large and valuable experience in the management of public affairs; and all that is known of his antecedents may be regarded as a guaranty for that confidence of the people who have elevated him to the Gubernatorial Chair by so large a majority. I bespeak for him your hearty co-operation in guarding and advancing the public interests; and I earnestly invoke Heaven's choicest blessings upon the people of Pennsylvania—that their abundance may never be diminished—and that her honored name may shine in the galaxy of the American Union with increasing splendor forever.

JNO. W. GEARY.

EXECUTIVE CHAMBER, }
Harrisburg, Pa., January 8, 1873. }

PARDON REPORT.

Report of pardons granted and death warrants issued during the year ending November 30, 1872, respectfully submitted for the information of the Legislature and the people of the Commonwealth:

1. JOHN LENNOX. Washington county. *Murder in the Second Degree.* May 25, 1867. Eight years in Western Penitentiary. Pardoned November 27, 1871. Recommended by Hon. W. M'Kennan, Hon. Geo. V. Lawrence, Hon. John Hall, U. S. marshal; Boyd Cummins, Janthus Bentley, W. W. Smith, C. M. Reed, J. M. Voyers, Wm. Wakman, W. C. Ramsey, sheriff; D. M. Donehoe, prothonotary; Samuel Ruth, clerk of courts; J. N. Hamilton, register; John P. Charlton, recorder; James B. Gibson, treasurer; S. M. Bell, Jos. M. Spriggs, J. W. Baker, Wm. Quail, Alex. Rankin, Samuel Ruth, W. H. Bradin, D. F. Patterson, Alfred Creigh, Samuel Fulton, John Allen, Geo. S. Hart, J. S. Hammond, Wm. Montgomery, Chas. C. White, Robert Wylie, Thaddeus Stanton, Jesse Jordan, B. F. Hasson, James S. Stocking, Wm. Workman, James Sterman, Chas. M. Rupple, Henry Gantz, the jurors in the case; Isaac H. Langdon, John Earwig, B. L. Craven, Thos. Warrell, James Brother, Wm. Lyons, George Hamlin, Joseph M'Curry, James Rainey, S. Mancha, Robert Orr and J. V. Rea. Reasons: Lennox has already suffered an imprisonment of over six years; he is now over fifty years of age and in failing health; the crime was committed during great political excitement, and under great provocation; the sentiment of the community in which the crime occurred is favorable to his pardon, and the ends of justice have been fully subserved by the punishment already inflicted.

2. BENJAMIN DILLEY. Luzerne county. *Keeping a Gambling House.* September 23, 1871. Fifty dollars fine and three years in Eastern Penitentiary. Pardoned November 29, 1871. Recommended by Hon. Thomas Collins, associate judge; E. S. Herriam, district attorney; I. M. Kirkend, mayor of Wilkesbarre; F. D. Collins and P. De Lacey, members of the Legislature. H. Armstrong, Hendrick B.

4

Wright, Rev. Thomas P. Hunt, Gen. E. S. Osborne, Charles Parrish,
W. H. Hibbs, E. J. Adams, E. J. Sturdevant, R. S. Hollingshead,
Wm. C. Yost, Charles Pike, R. J. Flick, John Faser, E. W. Sturdevant,
J. H. Flin, R. Bain, Edmund Taylor, A. B. Weil, Daniel Harkins,
Jonas Long, J. R. Coolbaugh, De Witt C. Cooley, S. Coben, A. Morse,
A. Hoffheimer, H. Ansbacher, and more than three hundred other citizens of Wilkesbarre. Reasons: Dilley never kept a gambling house ;
his offence consisted in allowing some persons, once only, to occupy a
room to play faro ; a conviction could not have been had with the facts
properly laid before a jury ; has hitherto borne a good character ; and
recent bereavements render his pardon almost indispensible.

3. JAMES WILLIAMS. Delaware county. *Assault and Battery.* November 27, 1871. One hundred dollars fine and ten days in county
prison. Pardoned December 1, 1871. Recommended by Hon. James
Pollock, George H. Stuart, W. J. Wylie, William Ray and others.
Reasons : He has always been a well disposed and inoffensive man ;
the assault and battery was provoked by gross and long continued
personal abuse. Fine paid ; imprisonment only remitted.

4. JOHN MAGINNIS, WILLIAM M'COLLEY, ABRAM HANES, JOSEPH
SNYDER, HENRY SEAMON, JAMES JACKSON and ANDREW SHEPPARD.
Philadelphia. *Assault and Battery.* November 2, 1871. Three
months in county prison. Pardoned December 6, 1871. Recom-
mended by John Wismer, Clement Wilson, Jeremiah Murphy, Wm.
Cooper, Charles Hard, Marshall Scott and John G. Gilliams, seven of
the jurors on the case; Hon. Leonard Myers, John O'Byrne, John
Lamon, Wm. R. Leeds, Joseph Moore, F. T. Walton, Albert Emerick,
William Montgomery, J. Swartz, F. B. Davis, Louis Schurk, Henssler
Horley, Kesler & Delancy, Thos. Oram, Henry Charlton, William
Oram, Isaac Bass, Edward T. M'Enau, William Murray, Henry
Mercer, S. H. Atkinson, Martin C. Cramp, Adam P. Hill, Robert
W. Dunlap, Wm. H. Weston, John Craig, John L. Stewart, Frederick
Shuster and others. Reasons: On the trial of their causes they
proved unblemished characters for peace, industry and sobriety ; the
evidence against them was conflicting ; they are yet merely boys, are
deeply penitent, and there are many extenuating circumstances connected with their offence.

5. DAVID JILLIARD. Wayne county. *Manslaughter.* May 9, 1868.
One hundred dollars fine and five years in Eastern Penitentiary. Par-

doned December 7, 1871. Recommended by F. B. Penneman, W.
Dimmick, A. M. Atkinson, C. B. Jadwin, E. A. Penneman, H. Wilson.
C. S. Minor, Geo. G. Waller, C. P. Waller, R. S. Dorin, Jno. R. Rose.
Samuel E. Dimmick, C. F. Elder, H. R. Beardslee, Geo. S. Purdy.
John M'Intosh, T. M. Crami, Thos. Collins, J. Robinson, Thos. J.
Walsh, E. B. Bumhard, Sydney Broadbent, Edward Sharp, H. J.
Kelley, and upwards of two hundred other citizens of Wayne county.
Reasons: The defendant did the killing in defence of his wife's honor ;
the deceased entered the house of the defendant partially intoxicated
and refused to leave when ordered to do so; that he used grossly in-
sulting language to the wife of the defendant, and, at least, twice
attempted to enter her chamber for the avowed purpose of committing
an outrage upon her person.

6. HENRY S. CORE and SAMUEL STAMBAUGH. Lebanon county.
Rape. November 19, 1870. One hundred dollars fine and two years
and six months in the Eastern Penitentiary. Pardoned December
15, 1871. Recommended by Hon. John J. Pearson, president judge:
Hons. John E. Kinports and Joseph Coover, associate judges ; Hon.
J. K. Killinger ; Jacob Shelly, Joseph R. Henry, Philip F. M'Cauley,
Samuel Beck, John H. Ulrich, Felix Light, T. T. Worth, W. M. Kauf-
man, F. A. Shultz, J. S. Shultz, Jas. E. Cherrington, Geo. M. Lininger.
W. Zimmerman, Samuel Shoop, Seth K. Smith, L. Z. Sack, J. M.
Zimmerman, W. E. Eck, M. R. Hunter, J. B. Shultz, E. S. Garrett.
Daniel A. Mizener, Elias Wallace, James Wallace, J. R. Henry, Philip
J. M'Cauley, Samuel Beck, J. H. Ulrich, Henry Kreizin, Samuel
Crause, D. Mosser, C. Woolison, P. Spangler, J. S. Mayer, J. H.
Weirick, J. N. Shirk, H. H. Carmany, F. Noll, W. D. Bassler, M.
Myers, J. Loose, G. W. Donges, W. H. Coover, and many others.
Reasons: Prior to the commission of this crime, the defendants bore
excellent characters ; public prejudice was greatly excited against them
at the time of their trial, and the testimony on which they were con-
victed was doubtful and contradictory ; and the facts do not justify
further punishment.

7. WILLIAM CLINTON. Allegheny county. *Adultery.* July 15,
1871. One hundred dollars fine and six months in county work-
house. Pardoned July 26, 1871, but fine not remitted. Recommended by Hon. Jas. S. Negley, Samuel Kilgore, Thos. A. Powley, A.
P. Logan, J. M. Creighton, Wm. B. Compton, J. P. M'Intyre, Joseph

Fleming, A. L. Pearson, Richmond Thompson, Joseph Brown, James Taylor, A. M. Brown, Richard Thompson, Robert Dickson, Patrick M'Gonegal, Charles Jeremy, S. Gillings, W. J. Hammond, J. A. Robinson, Thos. H. M'Ilvain, G. W. Schmidt, W. J. Anderson, W. J. Gilmore, W. J. France, R. H. Wilson, James Irvine, Jas. B. Hart, O. M. Barr, Thos. W. Davis, Wm. D. Taylor, J. E. M'Elvy, John Dalzell, Samuel B. Cluley, Chas. C. Small, Thos. D. Blair, Samuel Musgrave, Thos. J. Barbour, R. M. Crawford, W. J. France, D. Pancoast, D. Haworth, R. H. Wilson, Jas. P. Hoke, Hugh S. Fleming, and about one hundred others. Reasons: The defendant had always been an upright citizen; he has been amply punished for the crime alleged to have been committed; and Hon. Edwin S. Stowe, associate law judge, writes: " I believe Mr. Clinton has been sadly victimized by the father of this girl. * * * * I feel convinced, from what I have heard since the sentence, that the matter was only pushed on as a means, or because of a failure to secure more money."

8. SAMUEL W. FREEBURN. Dauphin county. *Obtaining Goods by False Pretences.* December 7, 1871. Six months in county prison. Pardoned December 23, 1871. Recommended by Hon. David Mumma, Wm. K. Verbeke, Rud. F. Kelker, George Bergner, Edward Birmingham, John Till, Richard Updegrove, P. H. Ryan, A. P. Erb, Wm. S. Shaffer, Dan'l A. Muench, Christian Heikel, sheriff; C. S. Funk, E. Byers, E. S. Zollinger, John L. Speel, Chas. H. Tunis, G. W. Simmons, James Nicholson, O. B. Simmons, John J. Shoemaker, John W. Young, D. Stockton, and F. K. Swartz. Reasons: The affidavits of Edward Martin, Amelia Hoke, and Rebecca Freeburn, state that the liquors for the purchase of which, through false pretences, the prisoner was convicted, were bought by him at the urgent request of the prosecutor, and that the prosecutor asked him no questions concerning any property of the said defendant, and that no representations were made by him that he owned any property. William H. Egle, M. D., prison physician, writes of the prisoner: "It is not probable that he would be able to serve out his time by such close confinement, and hence I earnestly recommend his release." Freeburn has since died.

9. BERNARD BRANNON. Philadelphia. *Burglary.* March 11, 1871. Two years in Eastern Penitentiary. Pardoned January 5, 1872. Recommended by Michael Meier, the prosecutor; Joseph H. Rheem, Thomas Kelly, Frederick Doner, Wm. Heckman, Thomas Cameron,

Jacob Koenig, John B. Winder, Garrett Vansant, Charles Hebsacker, Thomas II. Owens, and Wm. II. II. Wallace; eleven jurors; Hon. David Nagle, Aldermen Owen M'Donald and W. W. Daugherty, Henry Struble, T. A. Sloan, John Huplet, Joseph Pill, M. S. Bulkley, Francis M'Mannus, Geo. W. Williams, J. D. Williamson, Henry Christian, C. S. Peall, Edward L. Craft, Chas. II. Stokes, John W. Kester, Joseph II. Campbell, Edward K. Worrell, and many other citizens. Reasons: Brannon is a very young man and has always borne a good character for honesty; he is now lying dangerously ill, and the imprisonment already suffered is considered sufficient to satisfy the ends of justice.

10. MARTHA WESTON. Huntingdon county. *Selling Liquor to Minors.* January 11, 1872. Pardoned January 11, 1872. Recommended by Hon. R. Bruce Petriken, senator; Milton S. Lytle, district attorney; R. Milton Speer and W. II. Woods, counsel for the Commonwealth; M. M. M'Neil, A. Houck, D. R. P. Meely, R. M'Devitt, J. E. Smucker, George Jackson, A. B. Miller, J. Evans, Henry W. Miller, S. J. Lloyd, county officers; P. M. Lytle, Miles Zentmyer, R. A. Orbison, Jno. M. Bailey, J. R. Simpson, W. M. Williamson, E. S. M'Murtrie, D. Blair, Wm. P. Orbison, Wm. Dorris, K. Allen Lovell, and other members of the bar; J. L. Houck, Curtis Krider, Daniel Swartz, John W. Potter, John Ritter, J. W. Isenberg, B. S. De Forest, Christian Peightal, W. B. White, John Bolinger, M. A. Felmlee and Jacob Hoffner, the jurors who tried the case; J. B. Wakefield, Samuel Waters, G. W. Jeffries, Samuel Adams and John Lee, grand jurors; Wm. Brown, George Kyler, Thomas Dean, G. W. Johnson, and seventy other prominent citizens. Reasons: Mrs. Weston is a widow lady of great respectability; the business cast upon her by her husband's death, is her only means of support; would suffer by her imprisonment; there are many mitigating circumstances in her behalf; the costs will be heavy and the payment of them is deemed sufficient punishment.

11. SAMUEL BROWN. Mifflin county. *Burglary.* January 6, 1872. Fifteen months in Western Penitentiary. Pardoned January 12. Recommended by J. C. Bucher, president judge; A. Troxel, associate judge; II. J. Culbertson, district attorney; Andrew Reed, C. J. Arms, Joseph Alexander, II. J. Walters, J. S. Rakers, J. W. Parker, E. L. Benedict, J. B. Selheimer, D. W. Woods, George W. Elder, John A.

M'Kee, T. M. Utily, J. T. M'Clure, members of the Mifflin county bar; and Henry Bossinger, prosecutor. Reasons: The prisoner was found on the premises of the prosecutor, in the night time, in a stupefied condition, and made no attempt to run away or evade justice; he is of weak intellect, and a poor, needy, inoffensive man; the weak state of his mind goes far to take away the heinousness of his crime; the majesty of the law has been fully vindicated, and no good purpose would be subserved in further punishing him.

12. SYLVESTER GEORGE. Northampton county. *Larceny.* January 18, 1871. Two years and one month in county prison. Pardoned January 19. Recommended by the prosecutor, William H. Coleman; George W. Walton, sheriff; James M. Porter, district attorney; A. Meyers, S. M'Cammon, A. D. Shriner, O. L. Fehr, James J. Cope, George O. Walton, Martin Frey, George H. Young, and Uriah Sandt, county officers; B. E. Lehmer, W. H. Selfridge, Robert Peysert, Herman M. Fetter, James T. Borkek, C. A. Lubenbach, Larin J. Krause, R. S. Brown, George J. Desh, M. H. Snyder, D. D. Ritter, James H. Nolle, George Anawalt, J. J. Kechline, Jas. R. Roney, B. F. Boyer, H. H. Dash, Caleb H. Dart, H. P. Hammann, F. E. Lukenbach, E. P. Wolle, Theo. F. Severs, Jas. T. Brock, Jr., John B. Zimmte, R. A. Abbott, Geo. W. Reigel, A. N. Leinbach, Henry G. Borkek, Charles Kleckner, J. M. Seibert, Jos. A. Weaver, Jno. Lerch, and over one hundred other citizens of Northampton county. Reasons: The defendant is a young man who has hitherto born a good character; the crime was committed without felonious intent; the value of the property taken has been restored to the prosecutor. The petition of a dying mother for Executive clemency is granted.

13. PATRICK BURKE. Philadelphia. *Assault and Battery.* November 27, 1871. Two years in county prison. Pardoned January 19. Recommended by James Paul and Henry Wilhelm, prosecutors; John Russell, Isaac B. Smith, Edwin Markley, Ab'm L. Heebner, Emanuel Hess, S. Walkley, H. Heidrick and Lewis Thompson, jurors in the case; Geo. M'Gowan, H. M. Fetter, Samuel D. Strock, Jas. W. Marks, Adam Albright, Howard J. Potts, G. H. Griffiths, John Lamon, E. A. Porter, Geo. Handy Smith, Chas. H. Daugherty, Samuel D. Dailey, E. W. Davis, Frank S. Johnston, Wm. M. Randall, Geo. W. Fox, A. D. Levering, J. B. Hancock and Robert P. Deckert, members of the Legislature; Geo. W. Hammersly, William R. Leeds, J. C. Titter-

mary, James Givin, Hugh Collins, George Moore, D. A. Nagle, Edward G. Carlin, John F. Githers, T. J. Barger, Mackellar, Smiths & Jordan, Wm. Lang & Son, J. P. Delaney, James Hagan, Isaac M'Bride, A. W. Fletcher, C. J. M'Callister, Frank Register, J. D. Brooks, and many other citizens. Reasons: Burke has a wife and six children dependant upon him for support, who, by reason of his confinement, are left entirely destitute, and many other extenuating circumstances commend him to clemency.

14. PHILIP METZ and PETER LIERER. Erie county. *Arson*. June 3, 1870. Each one hundred dollars fine and three years in Western Penitentiary. Metz pardoned January 20, and Lierer, March 8. Metz's pardon is recommended by George Wagner and Michael Renz, owners of the building set on fire; Hon. S. P. Johnson, president judge; Thomas M. Walker, sheriff; J. C. Sturgeon, district attorney; E. S. Whittlesey, prothonotary; Isaac B. Gara, Geo. W. Colton, M. Schlaudecker, James Hunter, and many others. Lierer's pardon is recommended by Michael Renz and George Wagner, owners of the building set on fire; Hon. S. P. Johnson, president judge; Hons. Wm. Benson and A. A. Craig, associate judges; J. C. Sturgeon, district attorney; I. B. Gara, G. W. Starr, Chas. M. Lynch, O. Noble, M. R. Barr, John Clemms, C. P. Rogers, and many others. Reasons: The defendants were convicted upon evidence of a very doubtful character; testimony was produced at the trial proving an *alibi*; a large reward was offered for the conviction of the offenders, and an anxiety to have some person punished led to their being found guilty. They are mere boys; have always sustained good characters, and the law has been fully vindicated.

15. AUGUSTUS FIRCH. Erie county. *Arson*. September 1, 1870. Fifty dollars fine and three years in Western Penitentiary. Pardoned January 22. Recommended by Hon. John P. Vincent, president judge; Hons. Wm. Benson and Hollis King, associate judges; Wm. Carpenter, A. E. Shattuck, Jacob Frantz, N. C. Remington, John Sillyman, G. Van Court, John Fritz and C. M. Grearfield, jurors; J. C. Sturgeon, district attorney; W. S. Scott, O. Noble, S. Marvin, Jno. M. Hammond, Isaac B. Gara, J. Ross Thompson, Wm. H. Morris, P. Metcalf, W. S. Brown, M. B. Lowry, Geo. W. Colton, Jas. Skinner, G. P. Griffith, S. S. Spencer, John W. Hart, Wm. M. Gallagher, W. H. Lucas, D. B. M'Creary, J. W. Hays, James Dunlap, John Dunlap,

Jas. C. Marshall, Geo. M. Dunn and G. A. Allen. Reasons: Firch was convicted on the testimony of a single witness as to identity, who had never seen him before, and not until six months after the fire; petitioners believe the evidence was insufficient; affidavits attest his innocence; he has always borne a good character, and the facts do not justify a further imprisonment.

16. REV. E. W. KIRBY. Franklin county. *Adultery.* January 20, 1872. Two hundred dollars fine and thirty days in county prison. Pardoned January 24. Recommended by I. H. M'Cauley, Wilson Reilly, George W. Brewer, S. W. Hays, Hastings Gehr, Wm. M. Sellars, F. M. Kimmell, J. J. Eby, Lyman S. Clarke, J. M. M'Dowell, F. S. Stumbaugh, and T. C. Kennedy. Reasons: The defendant was convicted on very doubtful evidence. His imprisonment is not desired by the counsel of the prosecutrix and her husband. The disgrace attending his trial and deposition from the ministry is deemed sufficient punishment.

17. JOHN HASSON. Philadelphia. *Larceny.* November 8, 1869. Two years and six months in Eastern Penitentiary. Pardoned January 25. Recommended by Thomas Smyth, the prosecutor; Cornelius Bernon, Thos. Pauly, Charles Price, John A. Sexton, Daniel Lemon, Jacob Swartz, Timothy Fitzpatrick, James L. Robinson, John M'Ginley, Henry G. Filmer, William Newman and James Ogden, jurors; Robert P. Deckert, J. A. Houseman, Richard Peltz, Wm. R. Leeds, Isaac M'Bride, R. C. Tittermary and H. J. M'Intyre; for the reasons that the evidence upon which Hasson was convicted was not conclusive; he has served over two years of his term; his health is rapidly failing, and no good can result in his further imprisonment.

18. JOHN NEWELL. Allegheny county. *Mayhem.* July 8, 1871. Fifty dollars fine and sixteen months in Western Penitentiary. Pardoned January 26. Recommended by Hon. A. P. Callow, J. Morrison, Hon. James Blackburn, Joseph A. Butler, Jas. Prowden, James Lowry, Jr., H. B. Wilkins, Hugh S. Fleming, Wm. J. Diehl, A. L. Pearson, M. Swartzwelder, Wilson M'Candless, James A. Ross, John Glenn, C. L. Magee, John S. Lambie, Joseph Ross, Wm. J. Buck, L. E. Johns, W. W. M'Clelland, J. D. Mahon, James M'Gunnegle, Charles Jeremy, Samuel Hare, A. J. Jackman, Jr., Samuel M. Fulton, James Taylor, H. K. Sample, J. D. Fleming, W. M. DeCamps, M. S. Humphreys, John F. Edmundson, Thomas Steel, J. W. Kirker,

and others. Reasons: Newell committed the offence which led to his conviction, in a desperate conflict involving his life with a man notorious for his quarrelsome disposition and fighting propensities ; the evidence offered by the Commonwealth did not justify a conviction for any greater crime than assault and battery, and was of such doubtful character that the defendant was twice tried for the same crime before conviction was had ; the entire jury recommend his release.

19. HARRY SHEETS. Philadelphia. *Larceny.* August 18, 1871. Nine months in county prison. Pardoned February 1. Recommended by William Winters, the prosecutor ; Charles A. Porter, John Lamon and George M'Gowen, members of the House of Representatives ; Wm. R. Leeds, sheriff; Isaac M'Bride, Christian Kneass, Chas V. Mann, John V. Donnelly, R. C. Tittermary, R. H. Beatty, James W. M. Newlin, S. E. Beers, Geo. F. Hunter, E. R. Biles, and others Reasons : Sheets was led into this, his first offence, while intoxicated ; full restitution of the property stolen has been made ; he has a wife and child in destitute circumstances.

20. MARY MACOLLOUGH. Dauphin county. *Selling Liquor on Sunday.* February 2, 1872. Ten days in county prison and ten dollars fine. Pardoned February 2. Recommended by A. J. Herr, F. K. Boas, John H. Weiss, M. R. Young, Wm. Kuhn, Joseph H. Nissley, G. J. Kunkle, Geo. H. Irwin, Daniel Keyser, M. W. M'Alarney, Geo. Winters, David Mumma, J. S. Schminkey, Geo. M. Mark, J. C. M'-Alarney, Phil. Irwin, Samuel J. M'Carroll and Ovid F. Johnson. Hon. John J. Pearson, president judge, by whom the prisoner was tried and sentenced, and Hons. Isaac Mumma and J. D. Snyder, associate judges, has written that "she is a poor woman with four small children, who will suffer during her confinement in jail. We would be glad to see her relieved from imprisonment, and recommend that that portion of her sentence be remitted."

21. FERDINAND LE CLERC. Pike county. *Selling Liquor on Sunday.* February 22, 1872. Twenty dollars fine and ten days in county prison. Pardoned February 22. Recommended by Hons. G. P. Heller and F. R. Olmstead, associate judges ; John Klear, J. Halsted, J. M'Cauty, S. W. Drake and M. K. Rockwell, jurors in the case ; H. S. Mott, E. B. Eldred, Eli Cuddebeck, S. E. Dimmick, Jacob Kleinhaus, D. M. Van Auken, C. W. Ball and John Schimmell, M. D. Reasons: Le Clerc is a man of good character, and a respected mem-

ber of the community in which he lives ; he keeps a quiet and orderly
house ; the prosecution was malicious, and brought only for revenge,
the prosecutor having committed a gross assault and battery upon the
defendant, and been tried and convicted therefor ; he is advanced in
years, and of feeble health ; the jail of said county, from dampness
and other causes, is unfit for the confinement of a person in his state
of health, and his further imprisonment will be likely to result in serious consequences.

22. JEREMIAH FORCE. Allegheny county. *Selling Lottery Tickets.*
February 10, 1872. Five hundred dollars fine and six months in county
work-house. Pardoned February 27. Recommended by A. L. Pear-
son, district attorney ; Hons. Jas. L. Graham, Geo. H. Anderson, Miles
S. Humphries, Matthew Edwards, James Taylor and H. K. Sample,
members of the Legislature ; Thos. Mellon, Thos. Howard, Colonel
Wm. Philips, Thos. Steele, H. S. Fleming, S. F Von Bonhurst, W. C.
Moreland, John H. Kerr, Thos. W. Davis, Alex. H. Miller, Samuel B.
Culy, J. M. Gazzam, G. W. Coffin, James Rees, Louis Hoyer, M. D.
Peebles, M. H. Markle, Jno. A. M'Kenna, W. H. Maize, T. D. Williams,
S. A. Duncan, Jas. M. Fisher, S. L. Gibson, Henry Kane, W. H. Brown,
W. G. Stubbs, W. H. Lowe, J. T. Johnston, R. D. Holmes, Geo. Keyser,
Henry W. Barnes, J. S. M. Young, D. Fleming, Wm. M. Herron, and
other reputable citizens. Reasons : Force is sixty years old and in
ill health ; his physician, S. J. Furlough, has made affidavit that he is
suffering from a severe bronchial and lung disease and that close confinement will unquestionably hasten his death. He has always ranked
as a respectable and reliable citizen ; he did not think he was amenable
to the law, having taken out a license from the United States Government to sell lottery tickets. The prosecution was for the sole purpose
of extorting money. He has not engaged in the said business for
twenty months, and has entirely abandoned it. None of the facts in
the case justify a further imprisonment.

23. N. H. LONGABAUGH. Montgomery county. *Selling Liquor on
Sunday.* February 29, 1872. Fifty dollars fine and ten days in county
prison. Pardoned February 29, excepting as to fine and costs. Re-
commended by Andrew J. Sims, George W. Steiner, A. W. Dettra,
John C. Richardson, John Whitcomb, Jos. C. Beyer, William Stehler,
G. Henry Friend, L. W. Reed, M. D., Charles H. M'Coy, F. W. Bigomy,
M. D., Samuel Brown, Jr., Jacob Long, William Wood, and George

N. Corson. Reasons: No liquor has been sold at the defendants, hotel on Sunday; none has ever been knowingly sold to minors; complaint has never been made against him until now; it is believed the prosecution was instituted through malice, and the ends of justice do not require his imprisonment.

24. JACOB J. BAKER. Perry county. *Entering a Building with Felonious Intent.* November 2, 1871. One year in Eastern Penitentiary. Pardoned March 1. Recommended by Wm. Grier, John H. Sheibley, Dr. F. A. Gutshall, R. C. Adams, John Minnick, Benjamin Ritter, J. B. Froster, Dr. B. P. Hooke, Daniel Minnick, Sr., Andrew Kell, G. C. Palm, J. B. Miller, and nearly two hundred other citizens of Perry county. Reasons: Hon. B. F. Junkin, president judge, and Hon. John A. Baker, associate judge, state that defendant was induced to plead guilty under misapprehension of the discretion of the court, and that he could not have been convicted upon trial; he has always been an honest, upright man, and has a wife and two small children dependent upon him for support.

25. JAMES JONES. Lehigh county. *Larceny.* September 12, 1871. One year in county prison. Pardoned March 8. Recommended by Hon. A. B. Longaker, president judge; David Laney, associate judge; Jonathan Reichart, Wm. H. Hoffman, Stephen Kern, Jno. Strauss, Hiram Balliett, Thomas Jacoby, and Dr. A. J. Martin. Reasons: The prisoner is in ill health and subject to epileptic fits, which have increased in frequency and duration since his imprisonment; unless he is released, loss of reason and death it is feared may ensue; he cannot be relieved or benefitted by medical treatment while undergoing confinement, and clemency in his case would be an act of justice and humanity.

26. LOUIS WAELDE. Venango county. *Robbery.* January 28, 1871. Five years and one month in Western Penitentiary. Pardoned March 8. Recommended by Henry C. Johnson, S. Newton Pettis, C. R. Marsh, Thos. W. Graydon, C. W. Tyler, M. Park Davis, J. W. H. Reisinger, W. W. Deishman, Daniel Grubb, J. H. Beatty, Samuel T. Groff, B. G. David, Wm. Armstrong, Joseph Fox, E. H. Henderson, Alfred Zimmerman, N. S. Ernst, Harvey Sacket, A. L. Pearson, W. C. Moreland, and many other citizens. Reasons: Waelde has hitherto borne a good reputation for honesty; he was only accessory after the fact; he has made restitution of all that he received of the stolen property; upon the assurance that he would be exempt from prosecu-

tion, he confessed all he knew of the robbery and of the actual
offenders, and thereby was the means of advancing public justice.

27. LEVI RUSH. Allegheny county. *Selling Liquor on Sunday.*
March 12, 1872. Seventy-five dollars fine and ten days in county
prison. Pardoned March 14, excepting the fine. Recommended by
Hon. James Blackmore, mayor of Pittsburg; Hon. A. P. Callow,
mayor of Allegheny city; John A. Strain, Chas. B. Strain, J. A. Scott,
W. D. Moore, Thos. J. Keenan, Alfred Kerr, Alex. M. Watson, James
H. Kerr, S. H. Lyon, H. P. Miller, James M. Taylor, W. J. Asdale,
James Littell, W. H. M'Cleary, Joseph Brown, J. E. M'Elvey, J. C.
M'Carthy, and other reputable citizens. Reasons: Rush has heretofore sustained the reputation of a law-abiding citizen; the ends of
justice have been fully satisfied in the payment of the fine and the
punishment already inflicted.

28. MARY BOYLE. Chester county. *Selling Liquor without License,
and to Minors.* February 29, 1872. One hundred dollars fine and
sixty days in county prison. Imprisonment reduced to thirty days,
March 19, but fine not remitted. Recommended by W. L. Gray, J. L.
Torwood, John V. Sciper, A. W. Fairlamb, J. Morgan Baker, Perci-
pher Baker, James Lenny, G. W. Weaver, J. O. Dishong, Jr., E. C.
Smith, James Burnes, Wm. M'Candless, and fifty others. Reasons:
She is a widow, sixty years of age; has previously borne a good character, and proposes giving up liquor selling. J. T. Torwood, M. D.,
certifies that her health is very much impaired by debility and old age,
and that the imprisonment will seriously injure her and shorten her
life. This pardon is made in consequence of inequality of sentences
with other identical offences.

29. JOHN M'GRAY and JOHN O'NEIL. Delaware county. *Selling
Liquor on Sunday.* February 28 and 29, 1872. M'Gray one hundred
dollars fine and sixty days in county prison. O'Neil fifty dollars fine
and sixty days in county prison. Imprisonment of each reduced to
thirty days, March 23, but fines not remitted. M'Gray's pardon is recommended by N. J. Layton, John Lilly, Jr., Amos Gartside, George
Baker, W. Taylor, H. B. Taylor, George Robinson, Edward Lilley,
John Larkin, W. C. Gray, John E. Dyer, and many others. O'Neil's
pardon is recommended by G. E. Darlington, district attorney; W.
Cooper Talley, Y. S. Walter, Edward A. Price, John Hinkson, Samuel
H. Leeds, James M'Dade, Edward Barton, G. W. Weaver, Samuel A.

Dyer, John W. Gamble, Robert Hall, and many others. Reasons: M'Gray has always borne a good character. This is his first offence; and he has a wife and two children dependent on him for support. O'Neil has always kept an orderly house; he was not in the habit of keeping his bar open on Sunday. The reputation of the witnesses on the part of the Commonwealth is represented as very bad. He has heretofore occupied a good position in society, and his further punishment would answer no good end. This pardon is granted to equalize punishment for identical offences.

30. WILLIAM A. FARREN. Armstrong county. *Assault and Battery.* March 16, 1872. Four hundred dollars fine and six months in county prison. Pardoned March 27, excepting as to fine and costs. Recommended by ex-Governor Wm. F. Johnston, associate counsel for Commonwealth; David Barclay, counsel for prosecutrix; A. J. Montgomery, sheriff; Jefferson Reynolds, district attorney; E. S. Golden, associate judge; J. L. Conn, Wm. Reiber, Thomas Allen, Jas. M'Gee, D. J. Stewart, A. Campbell, Chas. T. Reynolds, O. D. Dyer, W. P. Book, G. C. Smith, W. H. H. Bell, and forty other citizens. Reasons: An affidavit of Henry M'Ghee, states that Farren suffered a terrible family affliction some years ago, since which time his reason has been impaired, and that from imprisonment his physical system is much prostrated, and unless he is released there is great danger that he may wholly lose his reason; and under all the extenuating circumstances mercy and humanity commend him to clemency.

31. ALEXANDER SIMPSON. Mercer county. *Arson.* September 26, 1871. Three years in Western Penitentiary and five hundred dollars fine. Pardoned April 4th, excepting as to fine. Recommended by Hon. John Trunkey, president judge; W. S. Eberman, sheriff; A. B. M'Cartney, Wm. Maxwell, N. W. Porter, Geo. S. Westlake, H. M. Hamblin, J. C. Brown, J. S. Graham, J. M'Kinney, P. R. M'Kinney, and nearly one hundred others. Reasons: Simpson was convicted principally on the testimony of the prosecutrix, who is very old and scarcely a competent witness; two others, on the same indictment with the prisoner, were acquitted; he is a very young man, and mainly the support of an aged mother; he has hitherto borne a good character, and grave doubts exist in regard to his guilt.

32. NEAL M'CALLION. Allegheny county. *Keeping a Disorderly House.* March 23, 1872. Three hundred dollars fine and nine months

in county work-house. Pardoned April 11. Recommended by T.
Tobias, M. Streny, John D. Nave, Robert A. Bell, Henry Ackerman,
A. H. Fisher, Wm. M. Leiton, T. A. Edwards, S. S. M'Kimmell, R.
Smith, Frederick Aines, Arthur M'Fadden, Thos. Connell, Jacob Anderson, Joshua Rhodes, J. L. Dillinger, H. W. Buffrem, R. M'Gowan,
David Danzeath, H. Brady Wilkins, W. C. Moreland, and many others.
Reasons: M'Callion's conviction was based on very doubtful testimony; he has always bore a good character, and the sentence was
extremely severe. His physician, W. V. Marquis, states that the
prisoner "has been an invalid for the greater part of the year and
will scarcely outlive his sentence."

33. GEORGE BROWN. Mercer county. *Murder.* April 24, 1869.
Eleven years in Western Penitentiary. Pardoned April 24. Recom-
mended by Hon. John Trunkey, president judge; Hons. David M.
Findley and John Lightner, associate judges; Henry M. Hamlin,
district attorney; I. M. Sheriff, W. M. Martin, I. H. Robinson, Robert
M. Walty, J. D. Moore, Jr., R. M. Irwin, R. H. Irwin, J. H. Rankin,
P. E. Shifler, W. A. M'Cormick, J. H. Mutter, J. G. White, Wm. M.
Robinson, W. M. Gibson, and nearly one hundred other citizens.
Reasons: Brown's health has become so much impared that longer
imprisonment will endanger his life; his conduct while in prison has
been good; he was only seventeen years of age when convicted; he is
the principal support of a widowed mother, and other circumstances
fully vindicate Executive clemency.

34. ALFRED COLLINS. Philadelphia. *Embezzlement.* November 22,
1871. One year in county prison. Pardoned April 25. Recommended by Eleanor Dean, the prosecutrix: Hons. Samuel D. Strock
and J. B. Hancock, members of the House of Representatives, from
Philadelphia; John Blond and William F. Moskey. Reasons: T.
Yale Smith, physician for the prison, states that Collins is dying of
disease of the lungs, and cannot live many days; his release is
prompted from motives of humanity, so that he may die at home at-
tended by his parents, who are worthy and respectable people. Since
reported dead.

35. JOHN LONG. Allegheny county. *Assault and Battery.* February 10, 1872. Six months in county work house. Pardoned May
3. Recommended by Hon. A. P. Callow, mayor of Allegheny city;
John Magran, Samuel Hastings, Wm. P. Hunskers, Louis Hilke, Wm.

C. Rea, Wm. C. Cook, and Joseph A. Drexler, members of police committee; Jacob II. Miller, Thos. M. Marshall, A. L. Pearson, and Thos. M. Bayne, and many others. Reasons: Long has always borne a good character; he has served on the police force with credit for several years; he has a wife and six children dependent on him for support; his wife is at times deranged and unfit to take care of the family; and all the facts justify the prisoners release.

36. WILLIAM PHILLIPS. Tioga county. *Assault and Battery with Intent to Commit a Rape.* June 2, 1870. Five hundred dollars fine and four years in Eastern Penitentiary. Pardoned May 3. Recommended by Hon. R. G. White and Hon. G. W. Williams, president judges; J. C. Strang, district attorney; Henry Sherwood and M. F. Elliott, attorneys for the prosecutrix; John J. Mitchell, and a number of the members of the bar; all of the county officers; several jurors in the case, and nearly three hundred citizens of Tioga county. Reasons: Phillips is quite a young man, and has always borne a good character; the circumstances justify Executive intervention.

37. GUY SMITH. Bradford county. *Adultery.* February 9, 1872. Six months in county jail and two hundred and fifty dollars fine. Pardoned May 4. Recommended by Hon. Ulysses Mercur, S. W. Alvord, J. P. Van Fleet, Allen M'Kean, E. W. Hale and E. W. Kinney; also J. L. Woodburn, D. L. Kepple, J. A. Neigh, J. J. Swartz, M. Stevers, Edward K. Salem and John N. Christian, seven of the jurors in the case. Reasons: Smith was convicted upon the unsupported testimony of the prosecutrix whose chastity is not above suspicion, and who is strongly suspected of having been improperly influenced to prosecute defendant; he makes affidavit that he never was guilty of the crime whereof he was convicted; the petitioners firmly believe him innocent, and the facts demand his liberation.

38. T. J. SPENCER. Warren county. *Assault with Intent to Commit a Rape.* March 6, 1869. One hundred dollars fine, and four years and six months in the Western Penitentiary. Pardoned May 4. Recommended by Hon. S. P. Johnson, president judge; Hons. S. S. Winnom and James Dennison, associate judges; Hon. Harrison W. Allen, Matilda Toby, the prosecutrix; C. W. Stone, L. F. Palmer, Robert Dennison, R. Brown, H. W. Jamison, Frank D. Reeves, G. W. Allen, Welbert Allen, R. B. Smith and numerous citizens. Reasons: Spencer's health has been broken down by his long confinement; his sentence

was very severe; having served over three years the ends of justice have been fully met.

39. JOHN GORE. Cambria county. *Murder in the Second Degree.* December 15, 1865. Fourteen years and nine months in the Western Penitentiary. Pardoned May 7. Recommended by Hon. D. J. Morrell, Robert W. Hunt, H. A. Boggs, Jacob Campbell, Cyrus Elder, Joseph Parks, A. C. Mullen, W. K. Pypher, Cyrus S. Pershing, Wm. Orr, John S. Rhey, and *all* of the jury who convicted him. Reasons: Gore had just returned from the army, and was under the influence of liquor when he committed the crime, and under great provocation; his health has failed, and he will die in prison unless released; the warden and chaplain of the penitentiary certify to his good conduct, believe him sincerely penitent, and recommend his pardon. Circumstances do not justify longer incarceration.

40. HUGH MARRA and JAMES DOUGHERTY. Philadelphia. *Assault and Battery with Intent to Kill.* November 20, 1869. Each one thousand dollars fine, and six years, eleven months and twenty-three days in Eastern Penitentiary. Pardoned May 25, 1872, excepting as to fine and costs. Recommended by James J. Brooks, prosecutor; A. Buzby, M. Elore, Geo. F. Kidd, Geo. Cryps, John H. Adamson, John Donaldson, Chas. R. Doane, Henry Kippleand and Phineas Lewis, nine of the jurors in the case; A. Welch, W. N. Oakford, Jas. S. Carter, M. Colm, D. H. Louderbach, Alfred Stimmel, W. W. Bell, H. Backroad, Harvey O'Neill, J. W. Dyer, Wm. Trappe, Chas. Hill, J. F. Reddy, A. H. Randall, John Scott, A. F. Young, J. R. Coxe, H. S. Jewell, W. H. Ward, Harry P. Stein, Wm. H. Anderson, Chas. W. Carrin, W. C. P. Coret, Jas. G. Weldon, E. Lehman, E. Klaglin, Whitney & Son, J. M. Smith & Son, Geo. J. Burkhardt, Ellis P. Moore & Co., Francis D. Pastorias, W. H. Robins, F. Widmyer, Wm. Ward, J. Beck, Chas. Woodward, E. L. Krider, Wm. W. Wallace, Henderson Young, Gaylord Harvey, Wm. S. Stover, S. A. J. M'Fall, Samuel Davies, E. Jones Lester, Chas. F. Hoyt, Geo. W. Fitzwater, Chas. Fitzwater, Nelson Brown, Daniel F. Morely, Robert Smith, W. D. Smith, J. M. Hammill, Robert Morris, Geo. C. Hammill, J. A. Longbridge, Hon. Robert P. Dechert, Hon. D. A. Nagle, J. M'Colgan, Chas. T. Burns, George Concannon, Chas. H. Dougherty, W. W. Dougherty, J. B. Delaney, Chas. W. Wilcox, John Parsons, Hart, Wallace & Co., and others. Reasons: It is represented that the conviction took place at a time of

great excitement and prejudice against the prisoners. The prosecutor, Mr. Brooks, in his letter requesting the pardon, says: "Learning that an effort is to be made to procure, from your Excellency, the pardon of James Dougherty and Hugh Marra, convicted of an assault and battery on my person, permit me to say I shall be gratified to learn that you have extended to them the clemency of a pardon." It was further represented and strongly pressed, that, by the pardon of these persons, information would be obtained of such a character as would uncover and bring to light numerous criminal offences against the revenue laws of the United States, and felonies against the laws of this State, and would greatly aid in the administration and furtherance of public justice. The punishment received by each is two years, six months and five days, the payment of a fine of one thousand dollars each, and the costs of suit.

41. HENRY PIFER. Westmoreland county. *Assault and Battery.* February 10, 1872. Two hundred dollars fine and six months in county prison. Pardoned June 1, excepting as to fine. Recommended by Alexander Kilgore, sheriff; Geo. W. Frick, J. M. Laird, J. H. Highberger, Wm. Deverter and Hugh Ryan, county commissioners; Peter Enset, H. P. Laird, H. Cop, Jonas Pifer, A. A. Stewart, W. H. Klingensmith, J. D. Gill, J. J. Johnston, J. C. Snodgrass, Jas. S. Moorhead, A. G. Marsh, W. Baughman, R. W. Singer, James A. Hunter, Eli A. Fisher, H. Kettering, C. H. Herber, George Dorn, S. L. Carpenter, I. W. Tarr, J. Gross, Hon. John Latta and C. F. Warden. Reasons: Pifer has, previous to conviction, always borne a good character, and this act was done under great provocation. The petitioners are confident in the belief that he will hereafter remain a good citizen; the punishment already suffered is considered quite sufficient.

42. MARY CORNELL. Erie county. *Burglary.* May 28, 1870. Three years in Western Penitentiary. Pardoned June 7, on recommendation of the board of inspectors of the Western Penitentiary. T. H. Nevin, president of the board, says: "The board of inspectors of the Western Penitentiary have requested me to apply to you for the pardon of Mary Cornell, from Erie county, Pa., sentenced May 28, 1870, for three years. Her sentence by commutation will expire January 28, 1873. She is 20 years of age. Her conduct has been uniformly good, we ask your clemency in her behalf because of her *very feeble health.* She will hardly live many weeks longer. The Sisters of Mercy

5

in Pittsburg will take charge of her if released, and care for her while she lives. I hope you will give this matter your immediate and favorable attention."

43. JOHN DOUGHERTY. Philadelphia. *Larceny and Carrying Concealed Deadly Weapons.* November 16, 1870. Four years in county prison. Pardoned June 8. Recommended by John Wilson, prosecutor; Isaac Clymer, Bernard Ginity, Wm. Shuters, Wm. A. Lamb, David Mercer, James W. Haig, John H. Reakert, Wm. Duberry, Lukins Tomlinson, Wm. Stenger and George Noble, jurors in the case; W. J. Pollock, Thomas Barry, James Givin, Wm. Groynn, M. D., Robert P. Dechert, Hons. Wm. S. Stokley and H. R. Kneass. Reasons: H. Yale Smith, physician of the prison, certifies that " Dougherty is now in *phthisis pulmonalis,* and will not live in prison half his unexpired term, and is confined to his bed and sinking fast." His conduct in prison has been uniformly good, and all the circumstances justify his release.

44. HENRY DORAN. Fayette county. *Murder in the Second Degree.* June 11, 1870. Seven years in Western Penitentiary. Pardoned June 8. Recommended by Hon. S. A. Gilmore, president judge; Hons. Alex. Cron and R. M'Cormick, associate judges; J. M. Ogleon, district attorney; J. K. M'Donald, prothonotary; D. Kaine, and over two hundred other citizens. Reasons: There was no intention on the part of Doran to commit a homicide; there was no ill-will between him and Lowe, the person killed; [Lowe began the fight—Doran knocked him down with his fist, and Lowe died in about an hour;] no weapon was used and the killing was accidental. Dr. John Boyd has certified that the health of the prisoner is in a critical condition, he having treated him for pleuritus, and then for phlegmonious erysipelas, complicated with other diseases. He is a young man, industrious and peaceful, and his release would be an act of justice and humanity.

45. CAROLINE BUPP. Perry county. *Larceny.* August 10, 1871. Two years in Eastern Penitentiary. Pardoned June 12. Recommended by Mrs. M. A. Bassett, prosecutrix; J. H. Graham, president judge; B. P. M'Intyre, district attorney; T. J. Sheibley, J. J. Sponeberger, D. Mickey, D. M. Rinesmitte, J. A. Magee, Hon. B. F. Junkin, Geo. F. M'Farland, J. W. Albright, J. L. Gantt, G. W. Ziun, Phil. Bosserman, Charles F. M'Junkin, J. Rinehart, J. R. Dunbar, Jno. L. Singer, R. L. Armstrong and many other citizens of Perry and Dauphin counties. Reasons: She has a family of six children, and upon her devolves the burden of their maintenance; three of the children

are too young to do anything towards their support, and one of them is an invalid; the sentence was very severe, and the ends of justice have been attained in the imprisonment already suffered.

46. MICHAEL DOEBLER. Lancaster county. *Robbery.* January 17, 1872. Five hundred dollars fine and four years and nine months in county prison. Pardoned June 13. Recommended by Frederick Myers, sheriff; D. P. Rosenmiller, Jr., district attorney; John W. Mertzer, prison keeper, and the entire board of prison inspectors; J. B. Amwake, D. W. Patterson, John P. Rea, Samuel H. Reynolds, H. B. Swarr, R. H. Long, W. W. Hopkins, Wm. Aug. Atlee, Chas. Pennes, O. J. Dickey, Emlen Franklin, P. D. Baker, and fourteen other members of the Lancaster bar; J. Kahler Snyder, Elwood Greist, A. S. Henderson, G. W. Krene, J. L. Kaufman, C. L. Hunsecker, P. B. Fortney, and many other citizens. Reasons: The facts elicited on the trial of Doebler scarcely justified a conviction and were not aggravated; the only testimony was that of the prosecutor, who was very drunk at the time of the alleged act; the entire jury have joined in the petition for pardon, stating that the facts were those of a drunken frolic and by no means justified the severe sentence imposed; the prisoner's character was always good and he has been sufficiently punished.

47. SAMUEL SAGE, WILLIAM SANKEY AND ISAIAH BELL. Lawrence county. *Burglary.* May 18, 1872. Each twenty dollars fine and six months in county prison. Pardoned June 15 Recommended by H. W. Boyles, the prosecutor; Hon. Thos. Pomeroy, associate judge; J. Davis, sheriff; S. K. M'Ginnis, prothonotary; Isaac Murdick, Jr., county treasurer; John W. Wallace, D. Craig, Sylvester Gaston, W. N. Aiken, S. W. Danna, C. M. Phillips, J. M'Michael, Rev. D. X. Junkin, A. P. Moore, W. C. Harbison, J. M. Lawrence, J. F. Johnson. John Young, John R. Pattison, John N. Enery, J. B. Hardaker, D. S. Clark, Hugh Flinn, John Mitchell, G. W. M'Cracken, Thomas Henry. W. P. Morrison, John M'Kinley, J. H. Gilliland, John Bower, and about four hundred others. Reasons: Two of the defendants are young men yet in their minority; they have hitherto borne irreproachable characters; one of them is the only support of an aged and infirm mother, a lunatic aunt and an orphan nephew; the offence was committed whilst they were under the influence of intoxicating liquors, and no serious damage was done to the proprietor of the store entered!

48. STEPHEN BONFIELD. Philadelphia. *Assault and Battery with Intent to Ravish.* October 1, 1870. Five years in Eastern Peniten

tiary. Pardoned June 27. Recommended by Hons. Robt. P. Dechert, E. W. Davis, D. A. Nagle and Chas. A. Porter, members of the Legislature from Philadelphia; R. C. Tittermay, Alex. M'Cuen, Jas. Given, Jno. F. Sharkey, Francis P. Haggerty, Geo. C. Barton, T. A. M'Devitt, Henry C. Hawkins, James T. Ford, W. H. Gilpin, James W. Latta, T. A. M'Clelland, Joseph F. Stockdale, John F. Glenn, John C. Lees, H. Hunter, James L. Clifford, and others. Reasons: Affidavits filed, state that the prosecutrix was a *common prostitute*, addicted to *habits of intoxication*, and a frequenter of the lowest haunts in said city; the defendant was tried on the woman's evidence alone, and if her character had been proven on the trial, he would have been convicted of assault and battery only; none of the facts in the case justify a further continuance of punishment.

49. ISAAC MORRISON. Clearfield county. *Murder in the Second Degree.* January 16, 1869. Seven years and six months in Western Penitentiary. Pardoned July 2. Recommended by Hon. C. A. Mayer, president judge; Wm. C. M'Cullough, district attorney; H. B. Swope, John Lawshe, Justin J. Pie, A. C. Tate, George M. Brisbin, C. Howe, J. B. Walters, G. Ashman, Millar M. M'Neil, R. A. Miller, Philip Brown, D. Caldwell, C. A. Willoughby, and many others. Reasons: Morrison has hitherto borne an irreproachable character; that the blow was struck in a moment of fear and without the slightest intention to kill or do great bodily harm; he has a wife and six children in extreme poverty; having served out more than half his sentence he has been sufficiently punished; he is predisposed to pulmonary consumption and cannot live much longer in prison; the prison physician, D. N. Rankin, certifies that he has several times been under treatment for hemorrhage of the lungs.

50. JOHN PRICE. Mifflin county. *Larceny and Entering a Shop with Intent to Commit a Felony.* August 27, 1870. Six years and six months in Eastern Penitentiary. Pardoned July 3. Recommended by Hon. Samuel S. Woods, president judge; Hons. Wm. Ross and A. Troxell, associate judges; J. S. Rakerd, district attorney; Elias Rheam, A. P. Mitchell, S. B. M'Arte, W. E. M'Dowell, D. F. Milliken, Isaac Strode, James Foust, John Calwell, J. P. Taylor, Wm. Wilson, L. A. Pollock and Charles Bratton, jurors; James Burns, G. W. Woods, R. W. Patton, J. Irwin Wallace, W. Johnson, J. S. Houtz, O. O. M'Lean, W. Irwin, and many others. Reasons: Rice was con-

victed solely upon the evidence of a woman of notoriously bad character, who, upon the testimony, was as guilty as himself; the punishment already undergone is sufficient, even if he was guilty; his health is suffering from confinement; the prison physician of the Western Penitentiary, to which he has since been transferred, certifies that he has required occasional treatment for palpitation of the heart; all the facts demand his release.

51. EDWIN KNIPE. Montgomery county. *Adultery.* March 1, 1872. Six months in county prison. Pardoned July 11. Recommended by Hon. H. C. Hoover, associate judge; H. M. Branner, district attorney; Rev. A. G. Werstner, C. H. Stinson, Henry Livezey, Joseph Ruch, David Jamison, Alexander Schall, Henry Acker, Jared Evans, Edw. Schall, Thomas C. Rambo, A. W. Corson, Jr., John R. Breitenbach, B. M. Boyer, H. L. Drake, H. T. Slemmer, Jr., Samuel M. Markley, and fifty others. Reasons: Knipe is a young man, has a wife and interesting family prostrated by his misfortune; he was convicted mainly on the evidence of Annie Long, the prosecutrix, a girl of exceedingly bad repute; the petitioners believe that conviction on her evidence is unsafe and improper; he has served the greater part of his sentence and the ends of justice have been fully attained.

52. HENRY WARD. Wyoming county. *Manslaughter.* February 2, 1872. Three hundred dollars fine and nine months in county prison. Pardoned July 15. Recommended by Hon. Charles R. Buckalew, H. Comstock, sheriff; E. J. Keeney, prothonotary; S. H. Sickles, register and recorder; G. M. Harding, president judge, Luzerne county; L. D. Shoemaker, Wm. Lilly, V. E. Piolett, John C. Bullitt, Geo. W. Woodward, A. Lathrop, Asa Packer, M. C. Mercur, W. W. Ketchum, Edwin S. Osborne, Hendrick B. Wright, Stanley Woodward, Henry M. Hoyt, E. P. Darling, T. A. Miller, R. P. Ross, E. S. Handrick, N. M'Devitt, H. Sherman, Cyrus Stark, P. M. Osterhout, F. C. Ross, C. P. Miller, D. D. DeWitt, S. Stark, James Kelly, F. C. Burnett, C. D. Gearhart, J. C. Wright, Thos. B. Wall, James N. Pratt, Frank H. Pratt, A. Day, and many other citizens. Reasons: The unfortunate occurrence which led to Ward's conviction was at a time when both he and Shaler, the deceased, were intoxicated. The relations between them had always been friendly. The shooting was purely accidental and without any malice, as stated by Shaler to his physician, Dr. Sayre. Affidavits of J. F. Rothrock, Edward R. Mayer and John V. Smith, physicians,

state that the prisoner is suffering from severe nervous prostration and partial paralysis, and his mental condition is such from his excitable nervous organization that unless released he will be a mental and physical wreck, paralyzed and insane for life.

53. FRANK STAPLEFORD. Lancaster county. *Robbery.* January 17, 1872. Four years and nine months in county prison, and five hundred dollars fine. Pardoned July 26. Recommended by D. P. Rosenmiller, Jr., district attorney; H. W. Graybill, Jacob B. Stehman, Henry Eckert, Lewis J. Kirk, Henry C. Herr, Henry Ammons, Jacob A. Buck, John B. Knox, Alvin King, A. P. M'Ilvain, John M. Hershey and John A. Stohler, all of the jurors in the case; Ezra Reist, Christian Gast, C. R. Landis, Lewis Speeher, Jacob S. Witmer and H. S. Musser, prison inspectors; John B. Warfel, D. W. Patterson, John M. Amweg, Philip D. Barker, H. C. Brubaker, Charles Dennes, Benjamin F. Baer, H. B. Swar, Samuel H. Price, B. F. Eshelman, A. R. Barr, Samuel A. Groff, Samuel Musselman, W. S. Shirk, Samuel Hess, Geo. F. Miller, Martin Stanton, and many others. Reasons: The prosecutor in the case was intoxicated during the evening the alleged crime was committed, and on the following morning could give no satisfactory account of his loss. It is believed that the evidence produced at the trial was not sufficient to justify a conviction. The defendant is yet in his minority; he has previously borne 'a good character; his conduct in prison has been uniformly good; he has a widowed mother dependent upon him for support; and no good can result from his further confinement.

54. ANDREAS MILLER. Allegheny county. *Larceny.* June 29, 1872. One hundred dollars fine and six months in county work-house. Pardoned August 10. Recommended by Hon. Edwin H. Stowe, associate law judge; Hon. James P. Sterrett, president judge; H. S. Baum, P. D. Piedmont, J. C. Hill, James Towell, John R. Baum, D. R. Kuhn, Edward Duff, Richard Thompson, George Reichard, Harry White, Joseph Irwin, John N. Berlin, John I. Marchand, Wm. M. M'Combs, R. D. Beatty, Alex. Bates, A. H. Gross, Albert Laufman, W. Lowery, Thomas J. Black, Thomas M. Bayne, and many others. Reasons: Miller has hitherto borne a good character; the jury recommended him to the mercy of the court; the petitioners believe him innocent of any intentional wrong; and he has a wife and family dependant upon him for support. Hon. Edwin H. Stowe, associate law judge, states that

if he had been on the jury he should not have convicted him, but did not feel there was sufficient cause to grant a new trial, and since the trial he has become fully satisfied that the sentence imposed by him was unduly severe, and should be remedied, and in view of all the facts in the case recommends a pardon.

55. JAS. S. BIRMINGHAM, ANDREW J. WHILTON, THOMAS H. GREAVY, THOMAS F. BLAKE, PATRICK CONLIN, DANIEL M'MULLIN, WILLIAM MANN, D. BUSHONG, DAVID BEAUCHAMP, HENRY CROOK, THOMAS HACKETT, JACOB WOLF, LOUIS PLANK, PATRICK DUGAN, JOSEPH SHEARER, TIMOTHY SHANNON, MICHAEL EUSTICE, ANDREW SPURLONG, JAMES SLADEN, JOHN BRISSETT and MODESTA BERGERON. Lycoming county. *Riot and Assault and Battery.* September 14, 1872. Birmingham, Whilton, Greavy and Blake each one year in Eastern Penitentiary. Conlin, M'Mullin, Mann, Bushong and Beauchamp, a fine of one dollar. Crook, three months in county prison. Hackett, Wolf, Plank and Dugan, two months in county prison. Shearer, ten days in county prison. Shannon, thirty days in county prison. Eustice, Spurlong and Sladen, twenty days in county prison. Brisett and Bergeron, mistaking the day forfeited their recognizances. Pardoned September 16. Recommended by Hon. A. G. Olmstead, Joshua Walbridge, A. Updegraff, A. J. Dietrick, S. G. Morrison, H. H. Martin and about two thousand other citizens of Lycoming and adjoining counties. Reasons: The defendants have heretofore been peaceable, industrious and law-abiding citizens; in this instance they were led into error and breaches of the peace in the exercise of supposed rights for redress of supposed grievances; they have expressed great regret and repentance; have already suffered much from confinement in prison before trial; most of them have wives and children dependant upon them for support; the laws have been fully vindicated, and no good could be accomplished by their further punishment. The following conditions accompanied the pardon: "It is hereby stipulated and declared that this pardon is granted upon the express condition that if any of the aforesaid persons, at any time during the several terms for which they have been severally sentenced, shall engage in or incite any riot, or aid in anything which by their assistance and countenance may terminate in riot, then this pardon shall be null and void and of no effect, and he or they so offending shall be re-arrested, and shall serve out, in the prison designated, the full term for which he or they have been sentenced, as herein before recited."

56. CHRISTIAN BINK. Dauphin county. *Larceny.* September 3, 1872. Six months in county prison. Pardoned September 16. Recommended by George Bergner, John E. Fox, John A. Smull, J. B. Boyd, A. K. Black and W. W. Jennings, prison inspectors; Dr. Wm. H. Egle, prison physician; W. K. Verbeke, mayor of Harrisburg; Geo. B. Swartz,˙Calvin Etter, Jos. F. Knipe, M. H. Lee, G. W. P. Davis, George W. Osler, and many others. Reasons: Bink is seventy years of age; his health is failing rapidly; being of unsound mind, his further imprisonment would deprive him entirely of reason, and also endanger his life.

57. CHARLES T. YERKES, Jr. Philadelphia. *Larceny and Embezzlement.* February 10, 1872. Five hundred dollars fine, and ten years and nine months in the Eastern Penitentiary. Pardoned September 27. Recommended by Hons. John F. Hartranft, R. W. Mackey, Leonard Myers, A. K. M'Clure, Thos. A. Scott, Wm. H. Kemble, W. W. Irwin, A. J. Drexell, Jos. M. Pile, John C. Bullett, Samuel Dixon, one hundred and thirty-three members of the Philadelphia bar, thirty-four members of the select and common councils, and many other citizens. Reasons: Yerkes has heretofore borne an irreproachable character as an honest and intelligent business man; he was in this instance convicted of a crime for an act done by his clerk in the ordinary routine of duties, and without the knowledge, much less any criminal intent on the part of the defendant; conviction was had at a period of unusual excitement in the public mind; the jury recommended him to the mercy of the court; two of the five judges composing the court dissented from the opinion of the majority, on the grounds that the crime of larceny had not been committed by the defendant, and that he had not been convicted according to law. The members of the bar petition for his release on the grounds of doubt as to whether he was guilty of any legal offence; and a due regard for the financial interests and prosperity of the city and other creditors calls for his release. The following conditions accompany the pardon: "It is hereby stipulated and distinctly understood that this pardon is granted upon the express conditions that the same shall be utterly void and of no effect if any money, fee, reward or compensation has been, or shall hereafter be paid to any person or persons for or by reason of any service rendered or supposed to be rendered in procuring this pardon, or for or by reason of any cause, matter or thing, touching or

concerning the same; and it is expressly declared and understood that the acceptance hereof by the said Charles Yerkes, Jr., shall be held and regarded as an adoption by him of this condition."

58. JOSEPH MARCER. Philadelphia. *Conspiracy and Embezzlement.* February 10, 1872. Three hundred thousand dollars fine and four years and nine months in Eastern Penitentiary. Pardoned September 27. Recommended by Hons. James R. Ludlow, Thos. K. Finletter and James Lynd, associate law judges; Hon. Amos Briggs, judge of district court; Hon. W. S. Stokely, mayor; Morton M'Michael, editor *North American and United States Gazette;* John W. Forney, editor of the *Press;* Charles E. Warburton, of the *Evening Telegraph;* Everett & Hinckens, of the *Sunday Dispatch;* Dennis F. Dealy, of the *Evening Herald;* Thos. Fitzgerald & Co., of the *Evening City Item;* J. W. C. Greene, of the *Sunday Transcript;* William Meeser, of the *Sunday Mercury;* J. M. Robb, of the *Age;* James S. Chambers, of the *Day;* Lenore and Blakely, of the *Evening Star;* John M. Carson, of the *Post;* and Peacock and Fetherston, of the *Evening Bulletin;* by numerous members of the bar of Philadelphia; by all the members of the select and common councils present at the meeting of March 28, 1872; one thousand and eighty-seven of the city police; one hundred teachers of the city schools; Hon. Leonard Myers, W. H. Kemble, L. Montgomery Bond, John Robbins, Egbert K. Nichols, Thomas B. Scarborough, Robert L. Bodine, Robert H. Pattison, W. H. Baker, E. J. Spangler, W. S. Fetter, Edwin Palmer, Richard F. M'Carter, Jr., Dr. L. D. Baldwin, Henry Budd, Simon W. Gorsler, John B. Moffett, Andrew J. Know, J. Alexander Simpson, George H. Mitchell, Rev. N. M. Price, Robert Betwell, J. Howard Wilson, Thos. Cochran, W. W. Harding, Dr. H. Ernest Goodman, and over nineteen hundred others. Reasons: No part of the moneys entrusted to the defendant were appropriated by him to his own use; he was the victim of circumstances, "a vicious practice having existed for years, which rendered it possible for any city treasurer to fall as defendant did;" the sentence is virtual imprisonment for life, and in conflict with the spirit of the Constitution, which prohibits the infliction of cruel punishments; his sufferings in mind, body and estate have been severe and unusual, and from the imprisonment will probably result in insanity. The following conditions accompany the pardon: "It is hereby stipulated and distinctly understood that this pardon is granted upon

the express conditions, that the same shall be utterly void and if no effect if any money, fee, reward or compensation has been or shall hereafter be paid to any person or persons for or by reason of any service, rendered or supposed to be hendered, in procuring this pardon, or for or by any reason or cause, matter or thing, touching or concerning the same; and it is expressly declared or understood that the acceptance hereof by the said Joseph Mareer, shall be held and regarded as an adoption by him of this condition."

59. JOHN ZEIDLER. Luzerne county. *Selling Liquor on Sunday.* September 18, 1872. Ninety dollars fine and fifty days in county prison. Pardoned September 27, but fine not remitted. Recommended by Hon. L. D. Shoemaker, W. W. Ketchum, Edwin S. Osborne, Alex. Farnham, I. Abrahams, A. J. Lengfeld, Robert Coover, Wm. C. Yost, H. Conrad, S. Franenthal, H. Wright, J. A. Merrick, P. DeLacey, H. Winton, J. A. Scranton, Frank D. Collins, Edward P. Kingsbury, Wm. P. Carling, E. L. Merriman, and many others. Reasons: Zeidler is a German, and kept a beer garden where families of his nationality were wont to assemble on Sunday, as is the custom in their fatherland, and being imperfectly acquainted with our laws, the defendant committed the act for which he was convicted; and the pardon was accepted on the following conditions: "It is stipulated and declared that this pardon is granted upon this condition, that if said Zeidler should be guilty of a repetition of the offence whereof he was convicted, that this pardon to be null and void, and he is to be subject to re-arrest and to imprisonment for the full term of his sentence."

60. PATRICK M'GINLEY. Montgomery county. *Assault and Battery.* August 24, 1872. Six months in county prison. Pardoned October 2. Recommended by Hon. John F. Hartranft, John W. Hullinger, Owen Cahill, Michael M'Dermott, John Heenan, J. Leedom, Charles P. Jordan, Charles Bradley, Edward M'Gaughey, Patrick Bradley, John Welsh, Edward Baxter, Daniel Wiley, Thomas M'Kibbin, P. D. Miles, Jno. H. Coulston, Daniel B. Yost, James M'Cormick, Hugh M'Lain, Michael Sheny, S. B. Helfenstein, Patrick O'Neill, John J. Norton, Stephen Mullen, John Gilmore, Samuel S. Townsend, and many others. Reasons: The evidence was insufficient; the identification of the defendant was incomplete, and there should have been no conviction; the offence was committed during the existence of a strike among and by the iron workers of the town, when there was considerable excitement; he is of good reputation for peace and quietness; is

the only support of an aged mother, a one-armed brother and two sisters; and it would subserve no good purpose to keep him longer in confinement.

61. PATRICK BROWN. Schuylkill county. *Murder.* September 19, 1870. Four years in Eastern Penitentiary. Pardoned October 2. Recommended by Hon. James Ryan, president judge; Charles D. Hipple, district attorney; Lin Bartholomew, prosecutor; nine of the jury in the case; Wm. J. Matz, Chas. F. Rahn, J. M. Glick, James Glenn, D. E. Nice, A. J. Huntzinger, A. P. Carr, M. D., Ephraim Philips, Clement S. Foster, Jas. J. Conner, Henry A. Moodie, J. H. Hoover, G. H. Helfrich, Richard Kuhn, and many others. Reasons: The evidence against Brown was only inferential, and if he had been alone upon his trial it would not have justified a conviction; the fact of his trial, conjointly with others, against whom the testimony was direct and strong, had a tendency to bias the minds of the jury; his character for peace and sobriety has been always uniformly good; owing to his delicate health the sentence is equal to imprisonment for life; he has a wife and four children dependent upon him for support; and, in consideration of all the facts, it would be injustice to continue his imprisonment.

62. FRANK ARMSTRONG. Philadelphia. *Larceny.* July 12, 1872. Six months in county prison. Pardoned October 7. Recommended by Hon. Thos. K. Finletter, associate law judge; Christian Knears, John P. Wetherill, James L. Claghorn, R. J. Houston, Joseph R. Chandler, and by the following citizens of Lancaster county: John W. Johnson, Wm. M. Slaymaker, G. W. Keene, S. L. Kauffman, W. A. Wilson, M. Brosius, Thos. B. Cochrane, A. S. Henderson, Jno. K. Reed, N. E. Slaymaker, Philip D. Barker, W. D. Stauffer and Ellwood Griest. Reasons: Armstrong is believed to be entirely innocent of any guilty intent; the crime was committed when he was supposed to be laboring under a mental alienation; his relatives and friends knew nothing of the offence until after his conviction; he is quite an aged man; he has heretofore maintained a respectable standing in society; his conduct in prison has been good, and the ends of justice do not require the fulfilment of his sentence.

63. A. F. BUTZBACH. Luzerne county. *Keeping a Disorderly House.* September 19, 1872. Two hundred dollars fine and three months in county prison. Pardoned October 15. Recommended by

Hon. Garrick M. Harding, president judge; Hon. E. L. Dana, associate law judge; Hons. L. D. Shoemaker and John Richard; Hon Ira M. Kirkendale, mayor of Wilkesbarre; W. W. Ketchum, Hendrick B. Wight, Henry M. Hoyt, H. W. Palmer, E. P. Darling, G. W. Kirkendale, Chas. A. Miner, M. J. Phiebin, G. M. Miller, C. B. Snyder, and many others. Reasons: Butzbach keeps a Beer garden, where a large number of respectable German citizens were in the habit of going, with their families, to seek recreation and enjoyment, after the manner of their people; the said garden has been kept in as quiet and orderly a manner as any in the country; the playing upon musical instruments was the chief cause of complaint, and has not heretofore been considered a nuisance in the community; the garden has been kept by the defendant in the same manner for five years and was never complained of before; the ends of justice will be better subserved by relieving him from imprisonment.

64. JOHN GRIMM. Allegheny county. *Murder.* October 23, 1869. Six years in Western Penitentiary. Pardoned October 15. Recommended by Hon. Thomas Mellon, the judge who tried the case; Hon. John M. Kirkpatrick, associate law judge; A. L. Pearson, district attorney; Thomas M. Marshall, prosecutor's attorney; E. S. Wright, warden Western Penitentiary; W. C. Moreland, Miles S. Humphreys, Jas. S. Negley, Jared M. Brush, Wm. Phillips, C. Barnes, W. N. Oliver, James Dougherty, S. B. Neely, B. F. Lloyd, Wm. F. Davis, Samuel Bridge, Jr., and many others. Reasons: Grimm has always sustained a good character; the offence was committed in self-defence; he served his country honorably and faithfully during the war; he has aged parents dependent upon him for support; having served out half his sentence the law has been fully vindicated and justice satisfied.

65. SEBASTIAN SEARLES. Union county. *Larceny.* February 21, 1872. Fifteen months in Eastern Penitentiary. Pardoned October 16. Recommended by Hon. J. C. Bucker, president judge; Hons. Jacob Hummel and Cyrus Hoffa, associate judges; J. T. Baker, Wm. H. Marr, Wm. Jones, Eli Slifer, A. H. Diel, Alfred Hayes, Jonathan Wolfe, T. Worrill Lynn, and many others. Reasons: On the night of February 12, 1872, two men, Wm. Hann and Wm. Richey, committed larceny in Lewisburg, and, on leaving town, fell in with Searles, who proceeded with them until arrested; there was no evidence that he had offered

any of the stolen goods for sale ; and the punishment he has already suffered fully answers the end of justice.

66. JAMES MEREDITH and JOHN RICH, (both colored.) Philadelphia. *Robbery.* December 22, 1869. Each five hundred dollars fine and four years and ten months in the Eastern Penitentiary. Pardoned October 17. Recommended by J. Gillingham Fell, for the reasons that the imprisonment already suffered is sufficient punishment for the offence ; they are mere boys ; that John Rich is feeble-minded, and is now in the hospital with his health much impaired ; their parents are respectable people ; their conduct in prison has been exemplary, and no good can result in their further punishment.

67. JOHN BARLOW. Luzerne. June 1, 1872. *Fraudulently Uttering and Publishing a Written Instrument to the Prejudice of Another.* Fine of two hundred dollars and three years in Eastern Penitentiary. Pardoned November 4. Recommended by W. F. Halstead, the prosecutor ; W. G. Ward, recorder of the mayor's court ; and Cornelius Ward and Matthias Gehen, assistant recorders ; A. B. Stevens, marshal of the city of Scranton ; J. A. Scranton, editor of the *Scranton Republican* ; W. W. Ketchum, Geo. Coray, J. H. Campbell, D. W. Connolly, M. J. Wilson, W. H. Gearhart, D. W. Rank, E. B. Sturges, C. Smith, Geo. S. Horn, A. Chamberlain, Geo. D. Butler, F. D. Collins, A. S. Hottenstein, M. W. Loftus, Thos. Dickson, John Raymond, John Holgate, and many others. Reasons : Barlow has made full reparation for the injury done, and paid the fine and costs of prosecution ; his wife is a lunatic ; he has hitherto sustained a good reputation for honesty and integrity, and no good can be accomplished by his further punishment. It is stipulated in his pardon that the same shall be utterly void and of no effect if any money, fee, reward or compensation has been or shall hereafter be paid to any person or persons for or by reason of any service rendered or supposed to be rendered in procuring this pardon, or for or by reason of any cause, matter or thing touching or concerning the same ; and it is expressly declared and understood that the acceptance hereof by the said John Barlow shall be held and regarded as an adoption by him of this condition.

68. JOHN PARKE. Chester, October 29, 1872. *Disturbing a Religious Meeting.* Twenty dollars fine and two months in county prison. Pardoned November 8. Recommended by all the members of the jury that convicted him ; Hon. Wm. Townsend, M. C.; Davis Gill, sheriff; Geo. F. Smith, district attorney ; Thos. V. Cooper, P. F. Smith, T. T.

Smith, Jas. E. M'Farland, Dr. D. W. Hutchinson, Wm. B. Waddell,
Rees Davis, J. Smith Futhey, Geo. M. Rupert, and numerous citizens.
Reasons: Parke is a hard working industrious man, and has a wife
and eight children depending upon him for support; he is what is
termed a "Loom Boss," and has charge of all the looms in the
Beaver Woolen Mills, and by reason of his imprisonment the opera-
tives of the factory are much impeded and may be thrown out of em-
ployment; Parke is a man very much respected and was unfortunate
in getting into company of others who were really the guilty parties;
there being no danger of a like occurrence on his part, the punishment
already inflicted is considered sufficient.

69. WILLIAM JONES. Philadelphia, May 23, 1872. *Assault and
Battery.* Nine months in county prison. Pardoned November 14.
Recommended by Charles Harris, J. B. Ascough, Matthew Corcoran,
J. H. Pauling, H. S. Cassel, A. C. Gill, B. K. Widler, John Chambers,
Wm. Watson, Chas. Godfrey and Thomas Armstrong, eleven of the
jurors who tried the case; R. W. Warner, Richard Ellis, John C.
Nipps, H. C. Dunlap, John Dumbells, Wm. J. Scott, H. W. Coupland,
Geo. S. Mellor, Frank Guynn, Jno. C. Thompson, W. Wilson, Chas.
W. Ridgway, W. F. English, J. H. Kennedy, and many other citizens.
Reasons: Jones has a wife and family entirely dependent upon him
for support, and whose condition is most pitiable; having been ill, his
physical condition demands his release; he has hitherto borne a good
character; his conduct in prison has been uniformly good, and all the
circumstances of the case call for his release.

DEATH WARRANTS.

1. GEORGE GRANT. Sentenced January 31, 1872, by the court of
oyer and terminer of Chester county, for the murder of Amanda R.
Spence. Warrant issued September 11. Executed at West Chester,
November 13, 1872.

2. MICHAEL MOORE. Sentenced September 4, 1872, by the court of
oyer and terminer of Cambria county, for the murder of Anna E.
Moore. Warrant issued October 11. Executed at Ebensburg, November 27, 1872.

TABULAR STATEMENT *of the number of pardons, (with yearly average,) and death warrants, issued from the year* 1791 *to* 1872, *inclusive, with the names of the Governors by whom they were issued, the population of the State at the time, and the approximate number of inhabitants to each pardon.*

YEARS, INCLUSIVE.	No. of years.	Population of the State......	No. of pardons granted......	Yearly average of pardons.	Death war'nts.	Av'ge approximate No. of inhabitants to one pardon.	BY WHOM ISSUED.
From 1791 to 1799..	9	434,373	1,188	132	10	3,300	Thomas Mifflin.
" 1800 to 1808..	9	602,365	1,909	212	10	3,000	Thomas M'Kean.
" 1809 to 1817..	9	810,091	1,555	172	6	4,700	Simon Snyder.
" 1818 to 1820..	3	950,000	1,304	434	6	2,200	William Findlay.
" 1821 to 1823..	3	1,047,507	787	262	4	4,000	Joseph Heister.
" 1824 to 1829..	6	1,200,000	821	136	7	9,000	John A. Shultz.
" 1830 to 1835..	6	1,348,233	502	83	8	16,100	George Wolf.
" 1836 to 1838..	3	1,520,000	481	160	6	10,000	Joseph Ritner.
" 1839 to 1844..	6	1,724,033	725	120	14	14,400	David R. Porter.
" 1845 to 1848..	4	2,000,000	327	81	11	24,700	Francis R. Shunk.
" 1849 to 1851..	3	2,311,786	378	126	6	19,500	Wm. F. Johnston.
" 1852 to 1854..	3	2,500,000	326	108	11	23,100	William Bigler.
" 1855 to 1857..	3	2,700,000	161	53	8	50,900	James Pollock.
" 1858 to 1860..	3	2,906,215	216	72	12	43,000	Wm. F. Packer.
" 1861 to 1866..	6	3,100,000	763	127	18	24,400	Andrew G. Curtin.
" 1867 to 1872..	6	3,650,000	425	71	23	51,400	John W. Geary.
	82		11,863	146	160		

www.ingramcontent.com/pod-product-compliance
Lightning Source LLC
Chambersburg PA
CBHW022143090426
42742CB00010B/1370